The Triumph Playbook:

---

7 Strategies for Overcoming Challenges in the Dark and Confidence to Live in the Light.

ALowe McCants

Contents

Dedication   4

A letter from Your Coach   7

Strategy #1 Get Over Being Hurt   11

Strategy #2 Give It To God   38

Strategy #3 Get Up   60

Strategy #4 Give God Praise   78

Strategy #5 Get A Team   93

Strategy #6 Give Your Testimony   113

Strategy #7 Get To Work   124

Final Run Through   130

Dedication

For My Matt and Sam

Thank you for your love. Your Greatness Constantly Inspires. I love you both so much.

For My Parents

Thank you for giving me Jesus.

& For You, I purposely wrote this book for You. The person reading, holding, or listening to this book. You, who faced life's many challenges in the dark. I see you. I've been you. The person you are, and wherever in the world you are. It is no accident that this book caught your eye. Maybe it was the intriguing smile on the cover or the engaging title. Either way, here you are. Reading my words, written purely to encourage you. As I look back over my life and through my countless journals, I see that the words that most inspired me came from the word of God. His words kept me. Guided me and became my strength when I felt I had none of my own. His words brought me hope and freed me. I have learned that God's words are true. The good and wonderful ones, as well as the not-so-favorable ones. **John 16:33** says, *"Know that in this world you will have trouble."* Life can be utterly brutal, sometimes. Certain situations can cause you to feel broken, confused, hurt, ugly, and less than useless. I know because I've been there.

But I'm not there.

This book is for anyone who has had a hard time believing the words that God has spoken over them. For those who have ever had to pick themselves back up again. For anywho who desires to no longer hide in the shadows. Those ready to boldly walk confident in their purpose, as the Light God designed them to be!

As a Marketing Strategist, I have learned the value of having a strategy for anything you want to achieve. Through the guidance of the Holy Spirit, I have discovered a 7-step strategy that will help you face the challenges of life head-on and come out Triumphant on the other side. This book is dedicated to you.

To YOU.

Dedication Request:

When this book blesses you, please share these 7 strategies with others going through tough times or before tough times happen. Give hope by sharing a copy of this book with a friend or small group.

Triumph is a noun that refers to a great victory or achievement, especially one that is achieved through great effort, perseverance, or skill. It can also be used as a verb to accomplish a great victory or success over an adversary or obstacle. Triumph can be joy, elation, or satisfaction from winning or achieving something significant, especially in adversity or difficulty. It is often associated with overcoming challenges or obstacles and can be a source of inspiration or motivation for others.

"But thanks be to God, who in Christ always leads us in triumphal procession, and through us spreads the fragrance of the knowledge of him everywhere." -**2 Corinthians 2:14**

A Letter From Your Coach

Hey You,

If you don't remember anything else from this book, I want you to know your worth and value in God's eyes. You are fearfully and wonderfully made in His image, with a unique purpose and assignment on this earth. You may have faced challenges and trials that have caused you to doubt your worth and question your purpose, but I assure you that God has a plan for your life, and it's a good plan. Jeremiah 29:1 says, *"For I know the plans I have for you," declares the Lord, "plans to prosper you and not to harm you, plans to give you hope and a future."*

My name is ALowe McCants, and I am a Servant of the who desires to help my brothers and sisters in Christ see themselves the way God sees them. I am a Confidence Coach as well as a Marketing Strategist. My journey taught me that our trials and tribulations were not meant to destroy us but to make us stronger and more resilient. The truth is You are no accident. You were born to Triumph.

In this book, "The Triumph Playbook: 7 Strategies for overcoming challenges in the Dark & the Confidence to Live in the Light, I share these 7 strategies that helped me overcome life's challenges and achieve my purpose. These strategies are based on biblical principles and personal experiences that have transformed my life. I also provide a guide to help you do some inner work to see where you are with yourself.

I believe that God speaks to us all, and it's my prayer that as you read this book, you will hear His voice speak to you. Pray that God will reveal Himself to you, speak to you, to help you understand and know your life's purpose. Remember, God is faithful and will answer your prayers in His perfect timing.

Now Guess what? Because you got this playbook, you just got me—your Confidence Coach. I love being a Coach because I love to see my clients win. When you win, We win. I am here to give you all the plays that helped me overcome some of the darkest times of my life. First, I need permission to Coach you. So, if I have permission to Coach you, say yes and sign your name here _____.

Now that I have your permission, Coaching starts now. I need you to commit to reading this book in its entirety. Decide now to read this short book through to the end. Because I want you to really win in life. I will challenge you.

After each chapter, there will be thinking questions, affirmations, and prayers. Answer those questions truthfully. Be honest with yourself. Read and speak the affirmations. Write them. Learn them. Of course, this is all your choice. I will not know whether or not you did, but I hope you do.

God has given me these 7 Strategies that all start with the letter "G." Yes, "G." One of my favorite phrases is K.I.S.S. which means Keep It Simple, Sis, Or Keep It Simple, Sir. I decided to keep it simple so that you can remember these plays when You're actually in the game of life and life starts lifein'. You know when stuff starts going crazy, and when the trials of life hit and make you want to hide in the darkness. Now you have this playbook to help guide you out of darkness into Triumph.

Read this book, apply what you read, and answer the questions with a sincere and honest heart. I know at the end of this you will find the strength and encouragement to live boldly as the person God created you to be – triumphantly bold in the Light. The choice is yours. With this book in your hands, my job is done. Now it's up to you to decide what to do with these words. I know it will be amazing.

Let's begin.

John 16:33 "I have told you these things, so that in me you may have peace. ... In this world you will have trouble. ... But take heart! I have overcome the world."

Strategy #1

Get Over Being Hurt

Now you see why I made you sign a mini waiver? As Your coach, I might not say the things you want to hear. But I have to keep it plain so you can understand quicker so you can walk in your purpose bolder. Listen, the first Strategy is a little straightforward and challenging to read. But the healing process can not begin until you are ready to identify the pain and accept that you no longer want it. I love the story in the Bible about the woman with the issue of blood.

In Mark 5, we meet a woman who had been battling with an issue of blood for twelve years. She had gone to countless doctors and spent all she had, but her situation only worsened. However, after hearing that Jesus was in town, though she was tired and possibly had given up all other hope, she pressed through the crowd to reach him. The Bible says that she thought that if she could just touch even the hem of his garment, she would be healed, so she pressed and reached out and touched the hem of his garment. As soon as she did, she was healed instantly.

What can this motivated Sis teach us about healing? What did she do? What was her breaking point? Who told her that Jesus' Clothes had healing capabilities? No one. She was tired of trying everything else and made it up in her mind that enough was enough. No one told her that touching Jesus' muddy pants would heal her, but she made it up, in her own thoughts. Your mind is a powerful place and the first place to look when it comes to healing and freedom to live a bold, confident life in Christ.

Proverbs 23:7 says, *"For as he thinketh in his heart, so is he."* The mind is essential to healing and obtaining anything. It starts with what you believe to be true. What you believe about yourself you become. Become the person who believes that Jesus is the source of your healing. And If you genuinely believe He is then you will seek Him.
 Just like this woman did after she decided that enough was enough.

I wonder what was it she heard that made her fully believe that He was enough. I wonder if she heard that Jesus had restored a man from demon possession or that he had healed a man with a shriveled hand in Mark 3. Either way, she was fed up, and knew that Jesus had to be the source of her healing, so she didn't give up. She didn't sit. She Got up. She pushed through. She decided in her mind and then acted on what she believed and her belief was enough. She was right. No one told her that it was his hem. She just believed that it was Him. If He could do it for others, He could do it for her. Good News Friend, if He could do it for her, He can do it for you. **Romans 2:11** says, *"God does not show favoritism."* He is faithful. He honors his word. He is a healer, and He desires to heal you. However, you can't heal whatever you are not willing to reveal.

Only you can feel your pain. You can explain your pain to others to the best of your ability, but only you can feel how intense it is. Only you can feel how real it is. Only you can feel your heart breaking, how deep cut truly goes. Pain is very personal. Two people could lose someone in their family. But that pain of loss affects each individual differently. Mainly because feelings are based on their relationship with their loved ones, as well as how they view those who have fallen asleep or have passed on.

People handle situations, life experiences, and pain differently. Its level of intensity is various, but all in all, it is unavoidable and yours. God allowed that thing, that hurt, that pain. For God is Sovereign.

Ephesians 1:11 says, *"In Him, we were also chosen,[e] having been predestined according to the plan of Him who works out everything in conformity with the purpose of His will, so that we, who were the first to put our hope in Christ, might be for the praise of his glory."* It is all for Him and in His will. Remember, if we are going to believe one part of the book, we have to believe all of it.

So here is the first real challenge. I want you to think of that thing. The thing that hurt you. The thing you don't fully understand. I hate taking you there, but we must reveal those things. Let's stop acting like what happened didn't, and let's acknowledge it.

They did hurt you...

That did break you...

That was embarrassing...

Whatever that thing is. I challenge you to say, "It was for my good." Because the truth is, It was sent to teach you something, show you something, reveal something, remove something, or something else good for you.

Romans 8:28 says, *"And we know that in all things God works for the good of those who love him, who have been called according to his purpose."*

This verse tells us that it is all working for our good. If you believe in God, you have to believe in His word. He said it is all for your good, including your pain. Therefore, when pain or heartbreak happens, acknowledge, feel, and embrace it. Learn from it. Ask, "What is this teaching me? What is this showing me? Where is the strength? Where is my Crown?" **James 1:12** says, *"Blessed is the one who perseveres under trial because, having stood the test, that person will receive the crown of life that the Lord has promised to those who love him."*

Once all of this is done, you must release it. Whatever it is, it did not come for us to hold on to it. We can not stop pain and hardships from happening, they are beyond our control. However, becoming unstuck is a choice that is within our control. And that process starts when we give up control to the one Who controls it all. But it is a choice.

Unfortunately, some people never get unstuck. Some people are just unaware that freedom is available to them. **Hosea 4:6** says, *"My people are destroyed for lack of knowledge."* Some people know that freedom is available but aren't willing to take the necessary steps to lead them toward freedom. Healing requires effort. Some people don't truly believe they are worth the effort. You know a person's truth by their actions, not their words. *oohhh that's good; highlight that.* Some slip so deep into depression after a trial that they don't realize that time has passed. They look up, and it's been days, months, and sometimes years have gone by, and they are still there, dealing with the pain that hurt left behind. However, I know none of those people are you. You are reading this book because you want to know how to take a licking and keep on ticking, how to remain Triumphant, and how to continue to thrive through it all.

But let me be clear, when You go through trials, It's ok to have a pity party. Be upset. God created our emotions for a reason. Embrace them. Feel the pain. Feel the hurt. Acknowledge what took place and what was lost. Take a moment. But Just a moment. **Psalms 30:5** says that "*weeping may endure for a night, but Joy comes in the morning.*" It is ok to take some time. Have a pity party if you want. Just do not change your address to pity lane. Do not live in pity. Also, don't allow how you temporarily feel cause you to make a decision with a lifetime of consequences. You have a message and story that is connected to someone else. Someone needs your voice. Embrace the new normal that the hardship left behind and decide to take your life back. This is your life, and happiness is a choice. Regardless of what is going on, you have a choice on what to focus on.

I know you probably wonder where Alowe gets off telling me to just "get over what they did to me." Listen, I can hear your thoughts as I type this, so now it's time for storytime. Because I honestly wasn't always this bold in my faith. But God allowed me to grow to this place. I could go back to my childhood and tell you about my rape, molestation, and how I almost failed the 8th grade because I lived in that shadow. My Parents didn't know at the time what was the cause of my behavior shift or what truly happened until I was older.

My preteens and teens were a tough time for me. However, my gift and passion for writing were born in that season. My parents were not too happy about my grades dropping, so I was put on punishment. No tv, phone, or radio, which was like my life back then. We didn't have the internet then, but I'm sure that would have been taken too, but that season led me to fall in love with books and writing poetry. I begin to fall in love with Maya Angelou's writings.

I even won my school's poetry contest where I recited "Still I rise." One of her more popular pieces. I begin to fall in love with words and filled notebooks with poetry. I read a lot of plays, which lead to my love of acting. The stage is like a second home to me now. A lot of who I am today and what I love to do was birthed through that season. Every season has a purpose. Nothing is wasted. God uses all of it. Has a plan for all of it. I can say that now with confidence because I kept going. Now I am able to look back and see how faithful God has been through it all of it.

Matt, my husband, and I tried for three years for our son Sam, and he finally came at the perfect time. Had he not come when he did, my life would be so different. At the time, I was around 273 pounds and 5'5", which was a lot of weight. I had no idea that I had gotten that overweight. Matt was playing for the Oakland Raiders, and we were so excited about his career! We loved being Raiders. We built beautiful relationships there. We had a wonderful family dynamic that still lingers to this day. We were going on our third year in Oakland and felt like we would be there for a while. Within the second month of my pregnancy, I discovered I had gestational diabetes.

I was crushed, however, Samuel saved my life. I had to live as a person with diabetes for the rest of my pregnancy. I was very disappointed. I had to prick my finger four times daily and gained a new love respect for those with diabetes. I also became more aware of my diet and how poorly I was eating. My diet had to change drastically. I was told that if I did not control my sugar numbers, my child might have type 1 diabetes. Unfortunately, despite all the changes I had made to my diet and exercise regimen, my sugars were still considered too high. I had to start giving myself insulin every night during the last four weeks of my pregnancy. I began to have panic attacks. I had a tough time giving myself the shot. Sometimes it would take me hours just to do it. I never really cared for needles and shots, and here I am being told to administer one to myself. I didn't care if it was a small needle. It was a needle. I have heard of people dying from mishandling needles, so needless to say, I had so much anxiety about it.

I was very stressed and anxious, which also increased my sugar number. My doctor kept warning me that stress was not good for my baby and me and was a part of the culprit in my numbers being high. I even would sometimes wake up Matt and ask Him to do it. I never let him. Looking back, I think I just wanted his support more than anything. When I got pregnant, I thought I would get to eat whatever I wanted and have the world bow down to me. Or at least that's how tv made pregnancy look. Wheww, not mine. Any of you who have ever had a baby knows everything we must go through to get those little humans here.

One day, My Mother and I were going to a birthday party for one of the Raider kids. She was in town because I would be induced to give birth the following week to our Samuel. They wanted to induce me because my sugar levels were high. My doctors were concerned that Sam would be born larger, so they wanted to take him earlier. I wasn't mad at that at all cause I preferred not to get all torn up. So we were planning for the arrival of Sam. It was the day after Thanksgiving. I will never forget this day. On the way to the party, I received the most sobering news.

To our disbelief and shock, Matt called and informed me that he had been cut from the Raiders. I was furious, sad, in shock, and in denial. My mom was driving because I was super pregnant a week before Sam's arrival. Thank God she was. I was in disbelief. I had to find a way to process what I had just heard and how to deliver the news to those whom I was 5 minutes away from seeing. I got that call when we were down the street from our teammates' party. I had to suck up my tears, bottle my emotions and tell my mom. She had a million questions. She usually does, but this time I remember not having any answers.

I had no idea what was going to happen next. We had made it to the party. We sat in the car for a few more minutes. We prayed and then walked in the door to see all of our now-former teammates. We had spent the last 3 years with these people, who were like family to us. A few of the wives met my mother and me at the door. I remember them hugging me and telling me that they were so sorry. It was so sad. It felt like someone had died. I remember brushing it off, putting on false confidence, and telling them I was fine to reassure them. Honestly, I was sobbing on the inside.

Each stage in the NFL has a process, and the cutting stage was no different. Because Matt wasn't vetted yet, he would be put on waivers, which means that since he's no longer a part of a team, he was free to be picked up by another. The team that is usually the worst gets first dibs on him. I was thankful for Him to have another possible opportunity, but I was having our child in 5 days. Our nursery was in Oakland. All of our stuff was there. We had made our home there. I was bringing new life there in Oakland. Sigh. December 1st was my induction date for the betterment of Sam and me, but it was now a strong possibility that my husband, the Father of my child, would miss his birth because of his job. If you're wondering if I was thinking all of this simultaneously, I was. I was an emotional wreck masked as a poster child for "Don't Worry, Be Happy."

I managed to tuck my feelings away for the time being. Matt came to join us at the party, and in a weird sense, that became our going away party. That was the last time I saw some of our teammates in person. The next day Matt got a call that he was going to the Cleveland Browns. He had to fly out within hours of receiving that call. After he left, I cried, prayed, and cried some more. I was so sad in bed waiting for his call. But God. When he arrived, he called me from there and informed me that he was heading back to Oakland to take me to the hospital. He told me that Cleveland was on a bye week and needed to sign his contract, but they were off for the week. Matt flew back to Oakland to be there with my mom and me for the 43-hour induction process. Samuel James McCants was born on December 3rd.

Nothing but God! Had he still been on the Raiders roster, he wouldn't have been able to be there for the delivery as long as he was. I really needed him and my mother. I ended up having an emergency C-Section. I was so thankful to God that my husband, my Love, was able to be there to hold my hand through truly a life-changing experience of bringing life into the world. God gave us a lot of favor at that hospital. We had a massive suite with literally 6 beds in it. All 3 of us were able to sleep in our own beds. Matt had to leave the second day after Sam was born to go back to Cleveland just to get cut because they needed another QB on the roster. He ended up finishing that season playing for the Chicago Bears. After a c-section, my mom and I had to pack up our apartment full of 3 years of stuff, ship the cars, and move back to Birmingham, AL. I had to keep it moving. I had to push through, but it was because I had learned to embrace the suck. I remember it being a slogan in one of Matt's books, which stuck with me.

Yes, it can hurt. It does hurt. Remember that God told us in His word John 16:33, that you will have trouble in this life. You will read that repeatedly throughout this book. It is a guarantee that I want you to learn to accept. Understand why troubles come. It is in the trials of life that produce the wisdom, strength, and fortitude necessary for your purpose. When they arise, acknowledge them, learn from them, and release them. Quickly if you can. So You can get back into the game of life. Your position, your life, and your ideas are necessary not just for your triumph but ours as a whole. I promise I didn't always have this belief. It was through yet another tough time that through me into hiding. That trial is the one that truly birthed this book. I want to share with you one of the darkest times of my adult life. Where I felt utterly hopeless.

Though Matt and I have been blessed with our Sam, I, unfortunately, have suffered miscarriages and infertility in my marriage. One day we told our family and friends that Sam would be a Big Brother. We had taken several tests, and they all said the same thing. Pregnant! We had believed that Sam being born broke the curse of not getting pregnant easily. Sam is a blessing. We had a lot of hope and excitement! Matt was playing for the Chicago Bears for the second time, but he was cut after the preseason. When it rains, it pours, as the old saying goes. We were now preparing for another move. We packed up our life yet again and headed back home this time. I will never forget that drive. I remember having a bad feeling about the baby I was carrying. I remember telling my friend I felt like I was going to miscarry. We had a lot of steps at the condo we were staying in.

I was about 12 weeks pregnant, caring for a very active 2-year-old. We had a move-out date, and we had to get stuff moved out on time so we didn't have to end up paying another month's rent. In my attempts to help, I remember carrying a mattress topper downstairs. It was heavy. I knew I probably shouldn't have attempted to take it alone, but I thought that if I slid it, it wouldn't have been that much for me to pull. Maybe I was wrong. I will never really know. This might be a bit graphic, and I apologize in advance if this is.

The next day, we were making the 10-hour drive home. I started bleeding. At first, it was light, and then it got dramatically heavier. I bled and cried the entire drive home. 10 hours straight. I was so sad. I felt so guilty. I cried when I got home. I called and set up an appointment with my doctor. Who confirmed we suffered a miscarriage. I cried more. Matt was so hopeful everything would be ok. That entire process broke me.

For weeks after that time, I found myself sinking further and further into depression. Here I am, with a two, almost three-year-old, and he demanded a lot of attention. They don't call it terrible twos for anything! He was running around everywhere, knocking stuff over. I was having such a hard time dealing with losing my baby, and I just didn't have the energy to keep Sam entertained. I felt so bad. I started thinking of everything: how Matt's career appeared to have ended; the death of my Father-In-Law; all of Matt's injuries; shoulder surgery, a dislocated toe, mild concussions, a broken leg; team after team; the moves and all of the broken leases; the money lost traveling across the country; the friendships lost, to even deeper stuff the molestation, the secret things I kept. It all hit me hard! I saw nothing but loss during this time, and it consumed my thoughts, which drove my emotions.

With so much happening, I sank into a deeper depression.

I was angry! I was angry with God. He was supposed to allow Matt to be a consistent starter in the NFL, a Hall of Famer. He was supposed to bless my womb with those babies. He was supposed to keep my husband from getting injured. He was supposed to protect me from getting raped. He was supposed to keep my best friend in my life. He was supposed not to let me have a high-risk pregnancy. So many things, I was angry!! I was tired of having to be strong. I didn't realize it then, but I was holding on to unresolved resentment toward God. This moment it was revealed how I truly felt internally about Our relationship.

I loved God, but I was Mad and had been for years. When I was depressed, and life pressed me down, what was inside revealed the damage I needed to take to God to heal. The pain I needed to release to get over it. In order to get over it you have to face it. Cross it. Face it to release it. See I was hiding it, even from myself. Acting as if what happened didn't. I needed to embrace it.

I was in the shower one day and was sad, I called out to God and said, "How long God will I have to deal with this? Are You done hurting me?" I heard Him ask "Are you done carrying it." Truth is what happened, happened. It was only still happening in my mind. The enemy wants you to keep looking backwards. When you look backwards, you focus on the things that have passed that no matter how much you think about them they will NEVER change. That thinking causes depression.

It was then that I realized that I had a choice. God started reminding me about how He held down Sam's birth. He began to remind me of how He got Matt into the NFL. How He has delivered me from hurt and lack of trust due to that rape. How He spared my life when I totaled out two cars. There was just so much to remember God in.

When You look back over your life, how can you not see God? See how those things bettered you, schooled you, equipped you, or prepared you. Those things contributed to who you are today. He had a plan for those things and He has a plan for now. He is the same God that promised to deliver you before and He is the SAME God able to help you through what ever hardship you might ever face.

God began to pour into me that day in the shower. I begin to hear His words so clear. The spoken word of God created everything you see. We were created in His image. Even though I was having difficulty believing God's words at the time, I started reading and turning scriptures into affirmations. I began writing my own affirmations and filled notebooks with them. The good happy, sweet, cute sayings...... I am strong, I am brave, I am peace, I am love... I Can do all things through Christ.

Before you knew it, I began to feel stronger. The words I was speaking started to affect my being. I was becoming wiser. I was created with power, just like you. When you remember Who's image you were created in. His words are the battery to our soul. Sometimes you just need a boost or a jump to just get you back on your way. Speak those words to ignite your strength, healing, understanding, and focus. His words are the source of it all. His Words give life to all things.

One day, I had to get up to fix my son a bottle, and it hit me. Maybe like it did that woman with the issue of blood from the Bible, but it finally hit me. I was tired of being depressed. It is time for me to get my life back. I was tired of being broken spiritually, tired of being sad. I was over staying in the house, eating, watching movies, scrolling on my phone, and letting life pass me by. I had to embrace what had happened, the losses, and what we had gone through and remember God's word. It was hard, but I decided to get up and move forward. The pain may not have been my fault, but the healing was my responsibility. I had to choose to get healed. I had to decide. Enough was enough. I started doing more than just speaking my healing. I decided that it was finally time to go get my healing. As soon as I decided I was over it I cried out to God who in turn said.

"Pruning is not punishment."

I was familiar with the concept of pruning, which is the act of cutting off dead or damaged parts of a plant in order to promote its growth and health. However, I wanted to learn more about why pruning is necessary. After doing some research, I discovered several reasons why pruning is beneficial:

Firstly, pruning helps to maintain plant health and aesthetics by removing weak or diseased parts of the plant, which can attract pests or hinder the plant's growth. Sometimes

God has to cut us to remove what is killing us. He might have to cut off some friendships, remove you from some jobs, break up some relationships to save you from the diseased that could have been passed to you if you were not cut away.

Secondly, pruning can be used to control the growth of the plant and its density. Sometimes God has to cut us down because we are getting a bit too big for our britches. Basically when we get a bit overconfident in ourselves. When we begin to reap the blessings from God and we forget the assignment from God. When we forget His way and start getting comfortable seeking our own way then. When we start growing in a direction, not in alignment it's pruning time.

Thirdly, pruning can encourage flowering and fruit production by opening up the canopy and allowing more light to penetrate. This stimulates the formation of flower buds aka growth. Sometimes God prunes us to help us to become more fruitful. When we go through trials we tend to run to God. When we go to God we receive His goodness, His freedom, His knowledge, and when we have more, we can give more.

Fourthly, pruning can be used to create specialized forms, such as hedges or boundaries.

Whew. Sometimes God allows us to be pruned to create boundaries. That cut was meant to teach you what lines need to not be crossed and why. Fifthly, pruning can help to rejuvenate old or overgrown plants by creating new growth and promoting more productive wood. I promise this is all on the Internet. Look it up if you don't believe me.

Finally, pruning can also be used to protect people and property by removing hazardous branches or limbs that could potentially cause harm to others. Sometimes pruning is necessary so that you don't harm others. Maybe you are going through a tough time and your mindset is off. He might have to cut you away from others so that you don't harm anyone else while you heal.

You felt pain because you were being cut. That cutting was just the pruning that God felt necessary for your survival. That's what He revealed to me. For no one prunes dying crops. But a Good Gardener will do everything in their power to make sure that their crop survives. God is a great and mighty gardener. He has you. He sees you. He has a plan for you so He is pruning you to perfect you for purpose.

Releasing pain can be challenging. It's not an easy process, but freedom from the trauma that hurt caused is attainable with work. When you are going through just keep going. The word says that our God is the same God. That if He did it before, He can do it again. Come on, Remind yourself that this has purpose too. Run the Play! Decide right now what to do with that pain.

Let's talk about it...

1.) What is it that you need to be free from or need to release? This is your book, so be honest. You can't heal what you do not reveal. Identify it. (hurt, betrayal, rejection, bully, hater, negative word, judgment, molestation, rape, storm, heartbreak, loss, breakup, sickness, etc.)

_____

_____

_____

_____

_____

_____

_____

_____

_____

_____

_____

_____

_____

_____

_____

_____

_____

2.) Go back and revisit the pruning process. Do any of those processes strike a cord with you? Do they feel like a process you have personally experienced?

_____

_____

_____

_____

_____

_____

_____

_____

_____

_____

_____

_____

_____

_____

_____

_____

_____

_____

_____

_____

3.) The enemy is clever and will want to try to make you shrink back and take up old habits. What are some things that you can tell yourself when the enemy tries to get you to fall back into harboring that pain again? This is Your book; speak to yourself in a way you need to hear. Encourage Your Future self.

_____

_____

_____

_____

_____

_____

_____

_____

_____

_____

_____

_____

_____

_____

Let's Pray:

Dear Heavenly Father, thank You for our life. Thank You for everything that You've allowed in our lives. You don't waste an opportunity to be glorified in our lives. So help us understand our pain differently, help us to see our pain the way You see it, and allow us to see ourselves the way that we know that You see us. We thank You, Father. We thank you, King, for choosing us to witness your Glory and Your Honor for Your name. Now help us, heal us today, help us to make the decision to release our heart, help us to make the decision to release our pain, help us to make the decision to release it all to You. We know that You are a healer. You are a deliverer. We thank You, Lord God, for healing us. Help us, God, to get over being hurt so we can take the necessary steps to move toward the beautiful purpose You have called us to. In the name of Jesus, we pray. Amen.

Affirm These:

1. I am Thankful for the life I have.
2. I release all things and situations that no longer serve me.
3. I have been chosen to give God the glory through it all.
4. I am Healed.
5. I choose to walk in freedom.
6. God is working all things out for my good.
7. It is well. I am Well. I trust God.

(Write this out in the space below)

Strategy #2

Give It To God

" Cast all your anxiety on him because he cares for you.."

1 Peter 5:7

I do not know why, but worrying about things is human nature. We want to think of every possibility and spend so much time sitting up and thinking of different scenarios in our heads. Like while driving, "Will this car crash on this road?" "Will this conversation make this person like me less?" "Will this outfit look cute on me?" "What are they talking about over there?" "Are they talking about me?" "She must not like me." "If they said that, it must mean this, or does it mean that?" Then sometimes, our worries are of more significance. "What's this lump on my breast?" "How am I going to pay my car note?" "Will I have enough money for my child's medicine and bills?" "I need a job. Where do I apply?" "Am I pregnant?"

This world is full of troubles. Full of things that could worry us, that do worry us. And there will, and there can always be, something to worry about. **1 Peter 5:6-7** says, *"Humble yourselves, therefore, under God's mighty hand, that he may lift you up in due time. 7 Cast all your anxiety on him because he cares for you."*

The first part of that scripture says to humble yourself under God's hand. That means that you must be willing to admit that God is in control of your life. He has the final say regardless of our worries. He is in control whether we acknowledge it or not. We must give up our desire to be in control of our life. We have to humbly be willing to accept all that He has for us. He is sovereign, honestly, whether you accept it or not. But life becomes sooooo much easier when you do.

Our worries can not change God's purpose for our life. Worrying literally does not change a thing but your blood pressure levels. I decided to look up the definition of worry.

Worry means to give way to anxiety or unease; allow one's mind to dwell on difficulty or troubles. After reading that definition, I realized that to worry is to give yourself into unease and anxiety. Like to worry is to give into an uneasy state and to welcome anxiety into your life. Worrying doesn't make anything better. It just welcomes more hell into your life. The Bible, though a profound book with passages that need to be reread over and over for understanding, makes it very plain how we should treat worrying.

Luke 12:25 *"Who of you by worrying can add a single hour to your life? 26 Since you cannot do this very little thing, why do you worry about the rest?"*

Philippians 4:6-7 *"Do not be anxious about anything, but in every situation, by prayer and petition, with Thanksgiving, present your requests to God. 7 And the peace of God, which transcends all understanding, will guard your hearts and your minds in Christ Jesus."*

Isaiah 41:10 *"So do not fear, for I am with you; do not be dismayed, for I am your God. I will strengthen you and help you; I will uphold you with my righteous right hand."*

Matthew 6:25 *"That is why I tell you not to worry about everyday life—whether you have enough food and drink, or enough clothes to wear. Isn't life more than food, and your body more than clothing? 26 Look at the birds. They don't plant or harvest or store food in barns, for your heavenly Father feeds* *them. And aren't you far more valuable to him than they are? 27 Can all your worries add a single moment to your life?*

28 And why worry about your clothing? Look at the lilies of the field and how they grow. They don't work or make their clothing, 29 yet Solomon in all his glory was not dressed as beautifully as they are. 30 And if God cares so wonderfully for wildflowers that are here today and thrown into the fire tomorrow, he will certainly care for you. Why do you have so little faith?"

Letting go or worrying sometimes is hard to do. Especially when you have been holding on to a thought for so long. When the pain and the hurt have become so familiar. The saying misery loves company is cliché but very true. (Misery that is a friend that's more like a wolf in sheep's clothing.) At first, it's so comforting that you don't realize how close you two have become. Time slips away, and you look up; hours have passed, and you have been lying in bed. Dishes are piling up. Laundry is all over the place, needing to go to the store but feeling so stuck. Stuck in that pain. Reliving the situation that brought on the trauma.

God promised to be our help in times of trouble. He is faithful, and He is always there.

We must call out to Him and trust that He is God enough to handle every problem. You have to begin to call out to God in your brokenness in the dark, alone- for YOU. Start praying more purposefully. Prayer is not just you speaking to God but Him speaking and revealing things to you. Prayer is 2-way communication with God. Use prayer to discover His voice.

1 Thessalonians 5:16-18 says, *"Rejoice always, 17 pray without ceasing, 18 give thanks in all circumstances; for this is the will of God in Christ Jesus for you."*

Verse 17 says to pray without ceasing. Pray in the shower. Pray while driving in the car. Pray while walking into the store. Before long you will have developed a habit of prayer. You will hear God speaking to you more clearly. And as you hear Him more your faith in Him will continue to grow, and with that comes understanding.

Another way to seek God is to get on the Bible app. Reading different plans. Plans about heartache and overcoming depression and hard times, or what ever topic you are currently dealing with. The Word of God truly has the answers. Though understanding it at first may will not come easy. The mind renewal process requires work. You have to work on it daily and often. Be very intentional with what thoughts you allow to linger in your head.

In **2 Corinthians 10:5b** it says that we must take captive every ungodly thought and make it line up with the word of God. Can you imagine catching all of your thoughts? Google says that your brain processes about 70,000 thoughts a day. And guess what the good book says capture them all and bring them back into agreement with the will of God. Listen, that requires skill and focus. You must find a way to be very sensitive to those worries and stinking thinking and choose to release them. You can change anything that you are willing to change your mind about.

So change your mind about your worries and concerns. Stop worrying and start seeking Jesus. He is in control, and if you are ever confused about your life, ask Him. **Daniel 2:22** says, *"He reveals deep and hidden things; he knows what lies in darkness, and light dwells with him."* So if you are in the dark, ask Him who will reveal what's happening. But you must cast those cares off and trust Him. Trust in His plan. The plan that He had for you before you were even born.

Jeremiah 1:5 *"Before I formed you in the womb I knew you, before you were born I set you apart; I appointed you as a prophet to the nations."*

Ephesians 2:10 *"For we are God's handiwork, created in Christ Jesus to do good works, which God prepared in advance for us to do."*

You are no accident. You are not random. I don't care what your parents said about how you got here. He sent you. You have to believe what He says concerning you. Trusting and having full faith in God can be your comfort when you know that He knows best. His best no matter what is for Our good. Trust the God You say You serve. Believe Him. Release to find your peace.

Jesus is the only source of everlasting peace, while the things of this world only offer temporary peace.Temporary peace and happiness are nothing compared to the permanent joy of God's presence in your life. The devil will put things in your way to distract you and take you off course. Our enemy is very clear on his mission and assignment.

Ephesians 6:12 " *For we wrestle not against flesh and blood, but against principalities, against powers, against the rulers of the darkness of this world, against spiritual wickedness in high places.* "

John 10:10, "The thief, comes only to steal and kill and destroy; I have come that they may have life, and have it to the full."

There is a real war going on over your mind, which is ultimately the war over your assignment and mission in life. The enemy can not possess you. You are possessed by the Holy Spirit. But he will try to confuse and distract you. How did he get Eve to fall? He challenged her mindset, and she didn't even know it. By what? His words. Be mindful of those who are speaking to you. The best way to triumph over worry is to always enlist God on your team. God not only has a plan for your life, but He literally can't lose. Now He operates on his own time and moves as he sees fit. He moves according to His will, so you must trust Him. His definition of time and ours is not the same.

Ask Noah, who was asked by God to build the first Titanic in front of his house, nowhere near the ocean, before there was even the technology to make such a thing. Talking about "rain was coming," something that no one had ever seen or heard of before. It took him 120 years to complete it. Can you imagine all of the emotions that he must have gone through? Can you imagine all the emotions his wife and children went through? And this was before there was access to the Holy Spirit. God wasn't just talking to everyone, so they thought Noah was a mental case. All the times he wanted to quit. Even though it took a lifetime, we learn that if God said it, it shall be fulfilled no matter the time frame. Further proving this point, **Isaiah 55:11** says, *"So shall my word be that goes forth from my mouth; it shall not return to me void, but it shall accomplish what I please, and it shall prosper in the thing for which I sent it."*

Begin familiarizing yourself with the promises of God. How can You lean on promises that You do not know? God also said we are destroyed for lack of knowledge. There are secret things of God that He is willing and eager to share, but you must learn to ask for them. **James 1:5** reminds us that God is a generous God who will give out His wisdom and other good things if we ask Him for them.

As a child of the Most High, your life is full of perks – both in the spirit and the natural. Growing up, My dad got asked to speak at many different events. I would attend my dad's speaking events backstage, meet the various speakers, eat snacks, and see how things were run. My Mom is an Insurance agent, and her company really knows how to party. We've been to Vegas and Bermuda and many events and concerts on State Farm's dime. They love my Mom. Those were privileges that I respected and always thought were cool. Sometimes I'd even bring a friend along.

Fast forward to me being a football wife, and that had perks, too. I'd get to walk on the field, walk around the facility and have access to an elite sisterhood that only those of us who are in it understand. So, of course, being a King's kid has its perks! A renewed mind, peace, joy, healing, salvation, strength, protection, and I could go on, but these are just some of the perks of being a child of the Most High God. Freedom from worry and "why me?" is available.

Im going to ask you this question. Why not you? Esther was tried. Joseph was thrown into a pit. Jacob got tricked. Abraham had to wait. Nehemiah had to serve. Peter had to fight. Daniel was lion food. Those 3 Hebrew boys sat in a fire. Job lost it all, I mean everything. Even Jesus himself was tortured. God did not spare His own son. We are joint heirs with Christ in Triumph as we as in His sufferings.

I'm going to repeat this because I need you to understand it. Memorize it. I'll give you another version this time. John 16:33 says, "I have told you these things, so that in me you may have peace. In this world, you will have trouble. But take heart! I have overcome the world." Taking heart means being encouraged. Have hope! Why? Having hope and remaining encouraged during a storm may seem complicated, but hard does not mean impossible. It just means you have to rely on His strength through His word and remember that He is within you.

Romans 8:17 says, "Now if we are children, then we are heirs—heirs of God and co-heirs with Christ if indeed we share in his sufferings in order that we may also share in his glory." I love this scripture because of its' comforting effect. It is an excellent reminder that God suffered yet rose victorious, which means that you and I will, too. We will go through and grow through every storm, coming out better than ever each time. Now, that is worth celebrating, right? So just trust and tap into your power source – our risen Savior. Renew your mind to understanding that He is with you and that is enough through it all.

Romans 8:28 says: *"And we know that in all things God works for the good of those who love Him, who have been called according to his purpose."* All things. All things. All things. The things we don't understand. Our hurts, our pain, our betrayals, our suffering – all of it has a purpose. God created us with a purpose, and our desire should be to fulfill it. We cannot walk boldly into God's purpose for our lives if we remain stuck in our storms. I need you to know that those things didn't come to destroy you. On the contrary, wouldn't they have succeeded if that was their purpose? Look at you. Conqueror, still here with another opportunity to lay your cares at God's feet to pick up His wholeness so that you are complete not lacking anything.

James 1:4 "Let perseverance finish its work so that you may be mature and complete, not lacking anything."

Trust that God is working this all out. He is preparing you so that you will continue to have all you need. Now here comes some more tough coaching. A part of releasing the pain is having to forgive the people who have wronged you. Whew…. now this is where I was almost out. Over time, I have actually grown to pray for the people that hurt me. I realize that they are people and they are human. None of us are perfect, and we all make mistakes.

People always categorize one sin as greater or worse than the other when the reality is – sin is sin. That's just how God sees it. When you realize we are all the same, all flawed, all learning, all doing the best we can, you learn how to give grace. In my maturity in Christ, I have learned to forgive them. When you forgive, you let it go and release the pain that haunts you. You tell yourself you're done with this pain, and you mean it, no longer allowing it to control your life. Forgiving them frees you from it.

As the scripture says: "Be ye transformed by the renewing of your mind...." I challenge you to recite this and make a habit of giving things to God. Let it go and leave it at His feet. Remember God's plans for your life and let it remind you that God is always the same – faithful and true. He can't lie, which means that despite what has happened, His plans are still to prosper you, not to harm you. All that you have or will ever go through is for your good and His glory. No trauma or obstacle can stop you from living the life God has promised unless you allow it to. If you stop believing and start doubting, you will begin to spiral downward like I did, but the Coach I am won't let you. Most importantly, God will not let you, just give your heavy load to Him, for with Him, it is light.

I know I know, I know. You still may not be ready to let go. Ask God to fully release your understanding of why certain things had to happen. Although I know it is all in His will, sometimes you just want to know why. I've been guilty of this a lot of times. Ask God to settle your spirit. Like I constantly have to ask Him to do for me. He promised to be our help, so trust Him. Trust whatever He has allowed. All is an inclusive word for everything. Good and bad is a myth. It is all God. It all has a purpose, and God has a plan that can not and will not fail.

Listen, I have been there. It can be hard to understand at times. Think of it like this – do you really know how your cell phone works? Nope. Or how a Microwave works. Do you really and truly understand how it turns cold things warm? Or a laptop, like how the screen projects light and words and sounds. Man, do you get the internet? Or Gravity? Like, think about that. You know what all of those are, and you probably use them all on a consistent bases. You didn't make them and don't fully understand them, but you trust them.

You trust your cell phone to make a call. You trust a microwave to warm your food. You trust a laptop with a ton of documents and personal information. You trust almost everything written on the internet. Yet you can't say you fully understand them. You just know it works. It's the same thing with our Father. Can you just trust Him even if you don't fully understand Him or His ways? Know that He is in control; whatever "it" is, it was designed for your good and His glory.

When you finally release It you are able to see God like never before. Trust God with whatever He allows. Settle your heart and mind. God is in it all. He hasn't failed you yet, nor will He ever. You are still here, so that means God has a great purpose for you and your pain. Your pain and your traumas are not supposed to be the end of your story. There are always two sides to it all. In all things, there is a negative and a positive side. It's all about what you focus on. Yes, you have been through some things. However, you went through them. Though awful, destructive, and painful, those things did not take you out.

You are a warrior, a living example of God's goodness. He has a plan for it all, which is more significant than all of us. He is much bigger than us and can see the whole picture. This is His masterpiece. We must move out of the way and allow God to orchestrate our lives as He sees fit. He knows better than us. We are not God, so let's, let go. Stop having to understand why and trust God with the "whys". And if you must know why, seek God, who wants to share His plan with you. The same God that got you in the game will be the same God that will keep you through it all. He promised to never leave us or forsake us. If we trust some of His words, we must trust all. Besides, we know He is not a man that should lie. He is the creator and author of our lives. He knows what role we were created to play better than anyone.

Lastly, remember that releasing the pain and granting forgiveness, even if not asked, frees you. Removing those worries that plague your mind into God's hands frees you from the fear and anxiousness that comes from reliving and overthinking. I pray you can start feeling comfortable giving God your cares, worries, and pain. The sooner you surrender to whatever God allows, the sooner you can return to peace and joy. It is all a choice, and it is all up to you. Know that God is standing by, willing and ready to take all your baggage, cares, sins, and mistakes and throw them into the sea of forgetfulness.

(**Micah 7:18-19**). It's incredible how God is willing to forget our mistakes, yet we hold on to them. God knew you would go through things that you would have hardships, but He never intended for you to carry them. You are so tired because you are taking something you were supposed to pass off. Friendly reminder again, You are not God. Stop trying to hold on to it all. Let those things go. Give them over to the Master. Look at your hands. God created you in His image but gave us little bitty hands. Yet He holds the world. It was never His desire for us to hold on to all of the things we are carrying. Give yourself grace, yet be intentional. This is all a process, but all in all, in the end, you will be better. Free. Lighter. You just have to take that step to let it go.

Letting go doesn't mean you forget. Letting go means that you release the pain associated with the situation. You release the desire to want to "get the person back." Vengeance is the Lord's. He promised to fight our battles if we just stand still and trust that God has a plan. It's one thing to say that God has a plan, but trusting Him is totally different. He says those who love me keep my commands. If we love and trust Him like we say, we should have no problem being obedient and accepting

His will. No matter what it looks like, no matter the situation, your faith in God can not waiver.

Sometimes I wonder "Is that why God allowed the trouble to come?" Was it to expose a hole in our faith? For I have learned that when something is pressed the inside is exposed. Either way, learn to see God's hand in it all. Learn it is what it is. Don't allow looking back to rob you of the present that is always in a hurry.

Thinking Questions:

1.) Write out the scripture 1 Peter 5:7 (NIV) and change the word "your" to "my" and the word "you" to "me" to make it personal. After you write it, read it out loud.

_____

_____

_____

_____

_____

_____

2.)List some current worries, cares, concerns, situations, people, and ideas you need to throw at God's feet?

_____

_____

_____

_____

_____

_____

_____

_____

_____

3.) Write a letter to remind yourself that God is in control. Include a scripture to encourage you that God is for you.

_____
_____
_____
_____
_____
_____
_____
_____
_____
_____
_____
_____
_____

Let's Pray:
Dear Lord,

Thank You for being such a loving God. A God who is concerned with all things pertaining to us. You know the number of hairs on our head and every cell in our body, and You have seen every tear we have ever shed. Lord, help us to always remember that You have an excellent plan for our life. Help us not forget that plan when we are hit by life's challenges. We are Your child, so we know the enemy will try to attack us. Help us remember that no weapon formed against us shall ever prosper. Remind us of your word that says that we have the victory! Help us to release these cares and concerns of this world, and help us to continue to trust You more. We love You and thank You for giving us peace and reassurance of Your incredible faithfulness.

In Jesus' Name,

Amen.

Affirm These:
1. I am NOT my Past.
2. I am free in Christ Jesus.
3. I cast my cares and anxieties to an incredible God who can handle everything.
4. I release pain and trauma and accept peace and joy instead.
5. I am not my mistakes.
6. I am willing and open to forgiving those who have hurt me.
7. God is my source of strength.

(Write this out in the space below)

Strategy #3

Get Up

This chapter is simple, yet it can be one of the hardest. I am about to challenge you! Get up! I'm not sure if you have ever seen Spike Lee's movie School Daze, but in the very last scene, Spike can be seen yelling at the top of his lungs, "WAKE UP!" That is me right now! "GET UP!!!!!!!" Stop lying around in your misery. Stop getting out of bed just to eat and use the bathroom. Go shower. Clean up the house. Put the chips down. Go for a walk. Get out of that familiar place of sadness and somberness. Get up and do something that a healed version of yourself would do.

What was your life like before the unexpected, life-shattering pain attacked and knocked you off your feet? That weapon God said would not prosper felt like it prospered a bit that day. Yes, that pain was real. You will never forget any of those unfortunate events, but they happened, and you nor I can change the past. All we can do is be in the now. Do what you have with what you have today. Be exactly where your feet are. Fight to stay present.

Winning through trials requires faith, and faith requires action. As the scripture says: "Faith without works is dead." Some like to say, fake it until you make it, but I want to say "Faith it until you make it." It's ok to not feel ok all the time. God gave us our emotions for a reason, and while I am not Him, I believe He allows our feelings as another way of teaching us.

Pain is a teacher. If you touch a hot stove and get burned, I bet the next time it's on, you will remember not to touch it anymore. Why is that? Because you got burned! Sometimes that pain is the only way we really learn. How many times have you been in a situation that you knew it was no good for you, but you kept returning to it. Like that delicious food that you over ate, or that relationship that you know is toxic but, for whatever reason, keeps pulling you back in.

Sometimes the pain is allowed to help us to learn. Yes, touching the stove is painful, but because you felt that pain, that will be a reminder the next time the stove is on. You will be more careful. Remember to look for oven mitts before handling anything on the stove. That was the lesson that pain taught. This proves Romans 8:28 that it all works for your good.

I get it. Pain is no fun, but just try and see it like this: when pain comes, purpose follows. Keep walking, keep going, and GET UP! In Luke 17:12-14, we read about Jesus healing ten men plagued with leprosy. Leprosy is a bacterial infection that attacks the skin. It is highly contagious. Read the story in Luke and look at what happened.

Luke 17:12-14, "12 *As he was going into a village, ten men who had leprosy[a] met him. They stood at a distance 13 and called out in a loud voice, "Jesus, Master, have pity on us!"*

Here we see the first and second strategies in action. Remember, the first Strategy is **Get Over Being Hurt**. Though the text doesn't entirely say so, these men were obviously over being sick. Could you imagine the suffering that they must have faced? The rejection from those in the community? Leprosy was not a hidden disease. It was highly contagious as well as an evident disease on the skin. And I bet it had a smell too.

They saw Jesus in the distance and started yelling at Him to have pity on them. They knew

He could heal them, so they called out to Jesus. **Give It To God** is the second Strategy in action. They sought out the Savior for their healing, which put the responsibility on Jesus to heal them. However, Jesus being the healer that He is, had to do something. What do you think happened next? I mean, you already know. They were healed, but how they received their healing was unique. Let's read on.

"*14 When he (Jesus) saw them, he said, "Go, show yourselves to the priests."*

And as they went, they were cleansed."

You see, Jesus didn't even touch the men. He didn't give them tons of medicine or rub them down with creams. He gave them a word, and they moved. His comment was "GO," which is your word as well – just GO! He didn't immediately heal them. It didn't happen in an instant for them. Their healing was attached to their obedience to move when God said move. Even in their still sickened state, God sent them on an assignment. Go back up and reread that last part in italics. Read it out loud.

"*And as they went, they were cleansed."*

Highlight and/or underline that. As they got up and were obedient, "as they went," they were healed. I'm sure they probably didn't understand why they needed to go to the priests, but they were desperate to be healed and trusted Jesus. They didn't argue and say, "But God, we are contagious... I'm still sick...why don't you just heal me now?" Imagine if they spent time asking questions, being doubtful, or even wondering if this would even work. Who knows how this story would have turned out. Their purpose was to get to the priests and be a witness of what obedience to God can do.

They became walking witnesses of God's goodness. People who saw them covered in sores, sickened, troubled, and embarrassed, now see them healed, clean, and joyful. Before the purpose came the pain. They were not fully healed when Jesus sent them and that is the secret as you go about your God-given assignment. You will discover all you need on the way. Your healing will be provided on your Journey. For it is healing within the Journey.

Matthew 28:19-20 says, "*19 Therefore go and make disciples of all nations, baptizing them in the name of the Father and of the Son and of the Holy Spirit, 20 and teaching them to obey everything I have commanded you. And surely I am with you always, to the very end of the age.*"

God has put us all on an Assignment, and it is to go! Teaching them what? What God has brought you through. To be an example of God's goodness. To teach one another. To help and inspire one another. For we are all connected and we will all face challenges, get knocked down, but as long as we breathing we have to keep moving. You have to get up. We still need you. Look don't overthink what God has in store for you. All those men did with leprosy after they were called by God was walk, and they were an example of God's goodness. Sometimes it's not about what you say as it is what you do. Just Be, Baby.

Whether you know it or not, there is someone who is depending on you now. You can help heal yourself and others by just showing up. Being honest and transparent. People need to see what strength and faith in the Lord looks like.

I know you are thinking, but how can I be strong when You feel so weak? **2 Corinthians 12:10 says**, *"That is why, for Christ's sake, I delight in weaknesses, in insults, in hardships, in persecutions, in difficulties. For when I am weak, then I am strong."* Basically, when you are weak, that is when you will see God's might and power step in. Less of you equals more of Him. As you ask to take on more of Him, you will take on more of His ways and wisdom.

The more you seek God and keep going forth in obedience You will begin to understand why certain things were allowed or needed to happen. God always has a plan. You must trust that and surrender your will or desire to sulk and stay down. You must get back up. Take a moment for yourself but don't let the enemy keep your message hidden from the world. Get up and go and be an example of God's goodness. The healing comes as you go!

What did getting up and going look like for me? For starters, I joined a gym, and what a blessing that place has been. I started working out daily. I went in there and paid for three months in total. I knew if I paid for it, I would commit to it. I ended up loving going to the gym. It was cool to just let go and forget about the miscarriages, how Matt's career ended, my broken friendships, the molestation in my past, and everything traumatic that had happened to me. The many secrets, the many things I was holding on to, I began to release as I began to work out. I had already mentally given them over to God, but the gym just distracted me, gave me something else to focus on. I ended up eventually getting a job managing the gym. Yes,

I was a manager at a gym, which still blows my mind. It would not have happened if I didn't decide to get up and take my life back. But that's not all that happened.

In 2020, Matt was a first-round draft pick for the XFL's St. Louis Battlehawks. God is so good! Matt instantly shined as a leader and was asked to be one of the Team Captains. He was honored, and I was ecstatic. Then, COVID took over the world and put us all on lockdown. The league was canceled, and they sent the players home. Matt was finally part of a winning team that had just made the playoffs, and St. Louis showed love too. They came out strong to support the guys and sold out every home game. They were about to open up more seating because the fan base had grown. Though it was short-lived, the experience was great for our entire family. Our son could see and feel the excitement firsthand at these games where daddy was playing, and mommy was cheering. It was a blessing.

After the league shut down, Matt was out of a job again. For weeks we had nothing to do. We were on total lockdown. We spent a lot of time together as a family and played a lot of Lego City. That summer, Covid hit our house. All of us had it. My dad had to be hospitalized. He was in there for 10 days with Covid and double pneumonia. That entire ordeal felt like it lasted for weeks. I knew God was not done with him. I was right, God came through again. Eventually, I started back working at the gym, and Matt began working out there.

He started to get to know the guys at the gym. Matt, nor I had any idea that these new connections were leading to a new purpose. When The owner of the gym was seeking to hire another trainer, I was quick to mention Matt. He became a trainer at the gym and loved it. Next, they decided to put on a combine for high school football players. They went around to all of the city's high schools, passing out flyers. Matt walked into a High School and got offered the head offensive line coaching job, and the following week, he accepted.

Matt coached there for about a month, and they won their Spring game. The O-Line absolutely dominated the field! The following week Matt got offered the assistant offensive line coach job at the school where we fell in love – The University of Alabama at Birmingham!

Listen, your movement can cause your entire household to be blessed! Movement doesn't just affect you it shifts the entire atmosphere. So now, may I ask, "Whose blessing are you holding up potentially in your own house because you are being too selfish to step out on faith?"

Wheewww... No, think about that. I have learned that God allows things to happen and allows us to be in certain situations, not just for us but, for others. We are the Body of Christ we are all connected to a bigger purpose. We don't need to overcomplicate our assignment. We just have to be who God designed us to be. To do what God created us to do. Then we can have the Triumph that God created for us to have. We just have to align with what has already been promised to us.

Jesus was asked once what the greatest commandment was? His reply can be found in Matthew 22:36-40.

"Jesus replied: "'Love the Lord your God with all your heart and with all your soul and with all your mind.'[a] 38 This is the first and greatest commandment. 39 The second is like it: 'Love your neighbor as yourself.'[b] 40 All the Law and the Prophets hang on these two commandments."

The greatest thing you can do to please God is love. John 14:15 says, "If you love me, keep my commands." What is the second greatest commandment? It can be found in verse 39. I will also retype it here to highlight it. "And the second is like it: 'Love your neighbor as yourself." If you love God like you claim, then You will love His people as He has commanded. He says that if you Love Him, you will obey His commands, so being the light for your peers is an act that proves that you are a child of God.

Matthew 5:14 says, "You are the light of the world. A town built on a hill cannot be hidden. 15 Neither do people light a lamp and put it under a bowl. Instead, they put it on its stand, giving light to everyone in the house. 16 In the same way, let your light shine before others, that they may see your good deeds and glorify your Father in heaven." God says that You are the light of the world. Yes, You. You were created to stand out. Be Bold, bright an attention getter, different.

We may all have unique assignments, but our purpose is the same. We are to prove that God exists, not by anything other than by our life, by being who exactly who God created us to be. Be you fully for His glory. We can't be the example and the light we are supposed to be if we hide inside our shells. Matthew says we are the city on a Hill, we could not hide if we tried. So stop trying. Your glow is vividly recognizable and so necessary. Everything about you is needed. So Shine. As we shine, we are to able see more clearly in the light. When we Shine, we help others as we help ourselves.

Highlight the following scripture and read it 3 times.

"I, the Lord, have called you in righteousness; I will take hold of your hand. I will keep you and will make you to be a covenant for the people and a light for the Gentiles, to open eyes that are blind, to free captives from prison and to release from the dungeon those who sit in darkness." –Isaiah 42:6-7

Reread verse 7 above. That is Your Assignment. You are supposed to shine your light so others can find their way to God. They are blind and they need Your light. I know you might feel overwhelmed at having such an incredible honor. Again, I will say do not overthink it here. All God asks you to do is live your life for Him. Give Him the glory in the good and the bad times. Know that He has His hands on you and will never give you an assignment that He will not help you with. Here is another favorite scripture that definitely applies, " *I can do all things through Christ which strengtheneth me.*" says Philippians 4:13. It Says all things. ALL. I can be such smarty pants sometimes, so I looked up the word all.

All refers to the whole quantity or extent of a particular group or thing." Similar words and phrases are; Every single one, total, utterly, each and every, in its entirety, everything.

So, no matter what the thing is, You CAN do everything you put your mind to with Christ. Here is the challenge: **#GetUp** and do something that the healed version of You would do. Go back to class. Go back to Bible Study. Take up a new online course. Post some new content. Put on some nice clothes and go shopping or to a nice restaurant. Go take some pics. Like to read books? Go to your favorite bookstore and pick up a new read. Buy another copy of this book and bless a friend.

Do Something. Commit to putting action behind your healing. I am not telling you to go back around places and people who hurt you or who do not honor boundaries. You cannot get healed in the same environment that got you sick. I am saying that recovery requires action. Take it slow but keep moving. You are necessary;

we are all connected to each other's story and growth. Remember that as long as you are walking in your purpose, God is faithful to provide everything you will need to succeed. You never know what your intention being fulfilled is tied to or who it's connected to. You could be the one to save your family. You could be the one to shift the atmosphere in your household. To shift, you must move! #GetUp

Ready to Move?

Let's Talk About You...

1.) What Gifts and Talents do You have? What do you like to do? In what ways can you personally show your light more?

_____

_____

_____

_____

_____

_____

_____

_____

_____

_____

_____

_____

_____

_____

_____

_____

_____

_____

_____

_____

2.) Are there any hindrances that keep you from showing up more? List them. What action steps do you need to take to remove them?

_____

_____

_____

_____

_____

_____

_____

_____

_____

3.) Write down a practical goal that you can commit to within the next 30 days? List the steps necessary to get it done. Pray and ask God for wisdom.

_____

_____

_____

_____

_____

_____

_____

_____

_____

Let's Pray:
Dear Lord,

Thank You for loving us so much that you sent us down here to earth on our own individual assignments, but our purpose is the same, which is to lead others to You. To show Your goodness on the earth, to show that You are not dead but very much alive, still capable and able to perform the same signs and miracles that you did in the Bible days. Help us to see how much our lives matter. Help us when things get hard and don't always seem to line up how we think they should. Remind us that Your ways are not ours, but You always work all things out for our good. Give us the wisdom we need when it's time to get up so we don't miss out on fulfilling our assignment. May we care about ourselves more to want to be able to walk boldly in our assignment.

In Jesus' Name,

Amen

Affirm These:

1.) I make peace with which I can not control.
2.) I trust God to be the guide of my life.
3.) It is NOT about me.
4.) My Story is necessary.
5.) My Voice Matters.
6.) I may get tired but there aint not quit in me I'm a King's Kid.
 I am a Warrior!
7.) I am Unstoppable.

(Write this out in the space below)

Strategy #4

Give God Praise

My father is the Head Pastor of The Guiding Light Church in Birmingham, Al. If you are ever this way, come by and worship with us. Every now and then I will open up service with prayer. I remember when I first started leading prayer, it was during Covid, our sanctuary was closed. It would just be a few of us. Honestly when I started, I was still broken on the inside and still secretly dealing with so much hurt. But it was then when I realized that through praying, praising and worshiping God, I began to feel free!

During those times of prayer, I didn't feel depressed or sad. I loved praying with others. I love being a part of their healing, and triumph. There is nothing like a person coming back telling you how God delivered them and thanking you for agreeing. Stuff like that makes you feel good. I feel like praying for others is a part of my purpose.

Though I started worshiping in my broken state, as I continued to serve God, I continued to heal, thrive, and get free. I could feel unspeakable joy, and whenever anxiety tried to rise, I would refer back to my now second-language prayer then praise the one who is able to fix it all. We were created to praise God. We were made for God to serve God, to honor Him. Psalms 22:3 says that God inhabits the praises of His people."

He literally comes and takes rest wherever His praises are ringing forth. And why do we want God near us? When He shows up, fear has to leave, sickness has to go, pain is healed, ways are made straight, wisdom is granted, and secrets are revealed. Like when God comes on the scene, He does not withhold anything. James 1:5 says, " If any of you lacks wisdom, you should ask God, who gives generously to all without finding fault, and it will be given to you." God is a giver. According to Psalms 84:11, He does not withhold good things from those who love Him. So if you desire anything, Praise God, let Him come down and see about you. When He gets to your house, hit Him for all you need: financial breakthroughs, healing, love, joy, clarity, peace. Then once you get it, go and be free.

Praise is Your purpose. By walking in your purpose, you will feel things falling off You. You will begin to refocus. You will start focusing less on problems and more on God. You will begin to focus on the promises. God promised to be a healer. He promised to be Your strength in hardships. Start thanking God in advance. Start saying things like, "Welp, here's another opportunity to see God." instead of, "Why Did this happen? Or why is this happening." Change your words. Change my mindset. Praise helped me to renew my mind. Giving God the praise through my gift of praying for others allowed me to remember Who we serve and how faithful He is.

Praising God literally frees you. Let's go back to that passage in Luke 17. Let's start with verse 14. Remember that Jesus has just healed the lepers, you know, the guys with the contagious, funky, rashy skin? He commanded them to go and show themselves to the Priests. He didn't touch them, nor did the scripture mention Jesus moving in that direction. He just gave out a call, and without question, the 10 lepers went through town to show themselves to the Priest. When they got there, they discovered they all had been healed. Let's take a look at what happened next:

"14 And when he saw them, he said unto them, Go shew yourselves unto the priests. And it came to pass, that, as they went, they were cleansed.15 And one of them, when he saw that he was healed, turned back, and with a loud voice glorified God, 16 And fell down on his face at his feet, giving him thanks: and he was a Samaritan. 17 And Jesus answering said, Were there not ten cleansed? But where are the nine? 18 There are not found that returned to give glory to God, save this stranger. 19 And he said unto him, Arise, go thy way: thy faith hath made thee whole." Luke 17:14-19

Wow, can you believe that only one of the 10 went back and thanked Jesus for their healing? Remember how they were all desperate for His attention? When they needed healing, they sought Jesus out. After they got their healing, they were content thinking that was all they needed and went on about their life.

One foreigner out of the group was the one that came back and thanked God. Now, of course, Jesus is God in the flesh, and God is all-knowing; and the text doesn't say, but I believe Jesus questioned him in verses 17 and 18 not because He didn't know the answer. He is God. He always knows the answer.

I believe Jesus used the situation to show the heart of God. As long as you praise and trust God, He is faithful to come and acknowledge you. To accept all those who call upon his name. All those who honor Him. He said He honors those who honor him, and that includes foreigners. That includes Blacks, Whites, Jews, gentiles, men, women, gays, straight, trans, cats, dogs, bears, and spiders. He honors Praise. His children were created to praise Him. Praise is what unlocks the door. It doesn't matter who it is. Or what You have done. God will accept You with open arms always.

In Luke 17:19, Jesus says something so profound that many people miss it. The Bible is so good because it is a book of puzzles and clues. My mind gets blown at how connected the scriptures are. They have many different authors but definitely the same voice. Ok, so Luke 17:19 says, pay attention and see if you catch it. "And he said unto him, Arise, go thy way: thy faith hath made thee whole." That was interesting to me when I read it because I thought he was already healed. Luke 17:15, " And one of them, when he saw that he was healed, turned back, and with a loud voice glorified God," So, He was healed. I went back and looked at what Jesus actually said. He said, in short, that because You came back and praised me for your healing, your faith has made you whole. There is a difference between being healed and being whole.

See, the other men got their healing from the disease they had. However, the man with enough wisdom to return and thank the Messiah was whole. So You know me, I looked up the definition of "Whole."

Whole – all of entire; in an unbroken or undamaged state; in one piece. Words that are similar are, enact, full, total, entire, and **complete.** Reading the word complete made me think of another scripture that mentioned being complete. **James 1:2-4** says, Whew, I love God, man. He leaves what I call breadcrumbs all throughout the Bible. Ok, read this.

*"Consider it pure joy, my brothers and sisters, whenever you face trials of many kinds, 3 because you know that the testing of your faith produces perseverance. 4 Let perseverance finish its work so that you may be mature and **complete**, not lacking anything."*

Let perseverance finish its work so that you may be mature and complete, aka whole.

According to this, Your praise has something to do with passing the test of perseverance.

A true believer lives in a state of gratitude. You praise and thank Him because you truly believe He is worthy of the praise. Luke 6:4 says, "4 For every tree is known by its own fruit." A child of God is known by what they do. God's child is always praising God because they know that it is all because of God's grace and mercy that we are not consumed. That we even get a chance to live.We know that God is in it all.

So what's the difference, according to ALowe, what she thinks whole vs. healed means. I believe the 9 were healed from that cycle. You know how some people who are addicts may get healed or overcome one addiction but end up in another? It because they didn't complet the cycle to move on. Its like Super Mario, in oder to get to the next level you have to beat the level you are on. Ok, Yall got me preaching, but God says that He is the Alpha and the Omega. That means the beginning and the end.

See the leapers in the beginning did right because they sought God. In the beginning. What they didn't do was choose to seek God out in the end. The didn't end off the cycle. I believe that's how we end up in cycles. Not allowing perseverance to finish its work. And since perseverance didn't finish the trial that was sent to complete you will return.

God allows this work to run its course because it is His desire that everyone be saved. I believe He will keep allowing situations in our lives to encourage us to value a relationship with Him. Trouble can come for a varies different reasons, but God allows some because we lack something, and the only way we can become complete is to enable the entire cycle to run.

So the one who received wholeness. I believe He was made whole because He has proven to have had true faith. When you have faith in God and trust and believe in God, you too will have trials and troubles; however, the difference is you have God on your side who promises you victory. Wholeness means completeness in Christ. Thanking Him in every season. All of the seasons are necessary. They all serve a purpose. The same is true for all of us. Your praise is an identifier of a true believer. A true believer does not need to be told to praise God, especially after a victory. A true believer knows it's all God. So, of course, they would Thank God for seeing them through.

Your praise is an invitation for God to come into your life and to show up and show out. Your praise shows that You trust God. You know and believe that He will come through for you just like He has for you before. Your Praise shows that you need God's help to obtain true joy, healing, and abundance. Your Praise causes the enemy to flee because Your praise brings God onto the scene, and we know that light and darkness do not mix. It must flee.

Your praise refreshes you, calms you, and reminds you that God is still on the throne and working on your behalf. Your praise encourages others to seek God. To desire a relationship with God for themselves. Your praise is necessary, and our God is so worthy. Your freedom is connected to your praise. Call God down where you are and see how the darkness instantly fades away.

Praise is the Cheat Code. You upset? Put on your favorite worship or praise song. Don't have one? Spend time looking up new gospel and Christian music. Go read the book of Psalms. The enemy is clever and will try to keep you from praising God because He knows that Your praise truly unlocks your power. Give God some praise today and every day. Don't just wait until Sunday when the worship leader tells you to raise your hands but dedicate some time today to praise and worship God for your blessings and things He has done. Praise Him for that pain too. Praise Him for it all, for He is truly in it all. Praise Him now for your TRIUMPH!

Your Praise is a weapon!

1.) What are Your Top 6 Praise and Worship Songs? Pick one song off the list and state why it is your favorite. What about the Lyrics move you? How do you feel after you listen to each?

_____
_____
_____
_____
_____
_____
_____
_____
_____
_____
_____
_____
_____
_____
_____
_____
_____
_____

2.) Fill up this space with everything you're grateful to God for. Call it a blessing list. I'll start it for you...

<u>My life, My Family, the air I am breathing</u>

_____

_____

_____

_____

_____

_____

_____

_____

_____

_____

_____

_____

_____

_____

_____

_____

_____

Thank God for it all

3.) Have you had a problem worshiping God in public? If so what was different? Why or why not?

_____

_____

_____

_____

_____

_____

_____

_____

_____

_____

_____

_____

Let's Pray:

Dear Lord,

Thank You for being such a loving and merciful God. Thank You for allowing us the opportunity to give You the glory and the honor, for it truly belongs to You. Thank You for praising You gives hope and reassures us that You are still God and that You still sit on the throne. Praising You reminds us of things You have done before. You are the same God. You are not like a man who changes constantly, but Your mind never changes when it comes to us. You love us wholeheartedly and want what's best for us always. Forgive us for not always seeing You in things and choosing other emotions when we should be choosing to praise You in it all. Grant us the wisdom to understand how our praise helps free them. For our praise invites you in, and where the spirit of the Lord is, there is liberty. Thank You for Your freedom and Your faithfulness. You are an amazing Father, and we thank You.

In Jesus' Name,

Amen

Affirm These:

1.) My Praise is a weapon.
2.) I am glad to praise the Lord.
3.) Praising God brings me peace.
4.) Praising God is connected to my wholeness.
5.) I am chosen to Praise God.
6.) My praise is valuable, and God listens as I speak of His goodness.
7.) Hallelujah Anyhow!
(Write these out in the space below)

Strategy #5

Get a Team

This strategy, right here, is one of the most important G's because your circle, your tribe, the people you call your team, are everything. Your family, of course, and Your spouse matter highly as you know. Please do not just be out here marrying and spending your life with just anybody. But we tend to take our love life a lot more seriously than those we call friend.

You need people. God created us for people, but we have to be careful because the people you choose to be around can affect everything. The right people around you can keep you encouraged and be your support in times of need. The wrong people around you can encourage you to do things according to their plans. Anyone other than God trying to be the Lord over your life is a distraction from your purpose.

There is only God's way, and the people around you have to be of the same mindset.

Being alone is not God's plan or design at all. So people in your life are necessary. A Team is essential. Genesis 2:18 says, "The LORD God said, "It is not good for the man to be alone. I will make a helper suitable for him." You can choose to do this life alone but remember God, your creator, straight up says it's not good for you to be alone. He also says that He will make a suitable helper. This is not just a marriage scripture. God has placed people in your life to help with your assignment. However, it is up to you to choose to allow people in your life. You can choose to have people in your life supporting you or choose to do life alone. Life is choice driven.

Ecclesiastes 4:9-12 says, "Two are better than one because they have a good return for their labor: If either of them falls down, one can help the other up. But pity anyone who falls and has no one to help them up. Also, if two lie down together, they will keep warm. But how can one keep warm alone? Though one may be overpowered, two can defend themselves. A cord of three strands is not quickly broken."

God says it's not good for man to be alone, and this verse in Ecclesiastes breaks down why. They will have a good return for their labor. My Mama used to get my brother and I up Saturday mornings to clean the house. She would always say, "Many hands, make light work." She was right. We could do more and finish faster if we worked together. The verse in Ecclesiastes says that if either falls, the other can help them up. In this world, we will make mistakes. Sometimes, we betray our faith and make decisions contrary to God's word. It's no secret that's why Jesus came and died so that His blood could cover our sins.

But when we make mistakes, we can lean on those around us to help encourage us back into the faith. Good friends don't let friends stray too far away from the faith. It says they will be able to keep each other warm. I like to think that they can keep each other encouraged. Life will hit you hard! Sometimes you are too busy choking on your own tears to pray. It's good to have people around you to lift you when you are weak. Encourage you when life hits. Remind you of God's word and help you return to the path toward purpose. It then says that one may be overpowered, but two can defend themselves. I don't know about You, but if my life is in danger, if I got to fight, I like my chances better of having someone have my back. Someone fighting with me increases my odds of coming out alive. When you are going through spiritual warfare, You need a group of people you can trust to pray with you.

A great team gives you accountability partners. It's easy to make a goal alone, and then if you give up, no one knows. You let yourself down, which should be the thing we don't want to let down the most, ourselves. Yet we do it all the time unaware, but that's a different book. When you include others in your life goals and plans, they can hold us accountable, check-in with us. That type of energy is so necessary.

Once You decide that you want to be free, to be healed, and to take your assignment seriously, there will be distractions. There will be opposition. The enemy doesn't want us to be great, to be free, to be whole. He knows that as soon as others get wind that you are no longer broken, operating in peace, they, too, will want to be free, healed, and whole. He wants to stop you. He wants you to get caught up doing other things and ignore what God has called you. He knows he can't take your life, so he will try to make you waste your life. He wants you worried about the wrong things, spending too much time watching tv and playing on your phones. He wants you to focus on everything other than God's plan and will for your life. When you have good people around you, however, they can keep you on track. They can look out for you and help you. God created us for the community, for each other.

When I finally felt like I was leaving my depressive state, I found myself online a lot. No one in my real world knew how sad I was. My phone did. Just like your phone knows all about you, what you google, what you look up, what advice you seek. At the time I was seeking encouragement. The internet provides a wide array of people going LIVE, sharing inspiration and motivation. I first found "Real Talk Kim." She is an incredible woman of God who used her real-life traumas to exemplify God's faithfulness.

Through her I saw a real example of God's mission for us in action. We are supposed to encourage others from our stories. Real Talk Kim definitely keeps it real! She openly shares her testimony of how she overcame drinking and partying, being divorced now 3 times, and other challenges. Her realism caught my attention. So raw, so real, and so necessary, she, too, is a Pastor's daughter. Her ministry helped me get out of my funk. God really began to use her to speak to me. She has a group called the inner circle. It's a monthly subscription, and I signed up. I loved being in the inner circle that was my first investment in myself.

One day I was on Clubhouse, in the room Millionaire Mastermind Room, and I heard Ash Cash Exantus. He is a financially motivating book writing Coach who later became my mentor, and we eventually partnered on a few different projects of his. Investing in these programs taught me the value of investing in my greatest asset, Me. God has blessed us with many gifts and talents, but what we do with them is up to us.

We have to be willing to go and polish our gifts. Perfect our skills. Sometimes that requires going to get a coach. Through those investments, I have found a team that has pushed, supported, and encouraged me like no other. They have become like family throughout this entrepreneurship journey. I met my business partner through that investment, and we are on a mission to help 100 Experts and Coaches reach 6 Figures in 2023. A goal I would never have thought or imagined, but it all started with seeking a team and getting in the right rooms and expanding my mindset. The thing about your mind is that once it extends it can't shrink back down anymore.

Working with Ash was a huge and incredible opportunity. I saw behind-the-scenes of the World's Greatest Money Mindset show on the Planet "Inside the Vault." As an associate producer for season 2, I got to coordinate the Money Reprogram event in 2022 with Ash and Jullien Gordan. I threw Ash a Birthday Party in NY from Bama. I got to speak on stages and at Masterminds because of that connection. I was able to meet some remarkable people and share the stage with some truly amazing people. But the moment that resonated with me the most was being able to be a part of the sales team where we generated over $10 Million in one weekend.

Listen. I can't unsee what I have seen. I know that God is real. I know what is capable. I have seen what faith and hard work gets you. Success is no accident. It leaves clues, and the clues become easier to identify when you get around the right people. All successful people typically do the same things. They make plans, and they execute them. Once you start hanging with the right people, you begin to have the right conversions. And let me tell you, all it takes is one conversation with the right person to change your life.

One of my favorite stories in the Bible is of Nehemiah. You can find his story in the book of Nehemiah. =) He was a servant called by God with no background in construction to quit his job and rebuild the torn down walls of Jerusalem, interesting choice to me because Nehemiah was no heavy lifter. He literally stood and held a cup by the King's side. However, God saw something special in him because He chose him. God uses whomever He pleases however He chooses. He qualifies the unqualified.

In Nehemiah 2, We see Nehemiah serving the King, but this particular day he was very sad, and the King took notice and asked what the matter was. See, Nehemiah had just heard that the wall back at this home town wall had been torn down. God placed it on his heart to rebuild the wall. Here is the King's response from Nehemiah 2:4-9

"The king said to me, "What is it you want?" Then I prayed to the God of heaven, 5 and I answered the king, "If it pleases the king and if your servant has found favor in his sight, let him send me to the city in Judah where my ancestors are buried so that I can rebuild it."

6 Then the king, with the queen sitting beside him, asked me, "How long will your

journey take, and when will you get back?" It pleased the king to send me; so I set a time.

7 I also said to him, "If it pleases the king, may I have letters to the governors of Trans-Euphrates, so that they will provide me safe-conduct until I arrive in Judah? 8 And may I have a letter to Asaph, keeper of the royal park, so he will give me timber to make beams for the gates of the citadel by the temple and for the city wall and for the residence I will occupy?" And because the gracious hand of my God was on me, the king granted my requests. 9 So I went to the governors of Trans-Euphrates and gave them the king's letters. The king had also sent army officers and cavalry with me."

Do you see how Nehemiah was blessed because he served the right person? The King set him up with all the tools he needed to build the wall, the tools to build a house to live in when he got there, an army to escort him on his way and allowed him to take off all the time he needed. Proverbs 18:16 says, " Giving a gift can open doors; it gives access to important people!" that access comes with perks. When God rewards you with the opportunity to be in the rooms with the great, take the time to see how you can help them. How can your gift make the room better? A gift is never for the one who is giving it. Help someone else. Go into these places to see what solution you can bring, and you will open yourself up to learning and growing with those you align with. Just because your millions haven't hit yet, doesn't make you any less a multi-millionaire. There used to be a saying that if you hang around five wealthy people, you will become the 6th.

Until then, find a way to serve them because the only broke people around them are serving them until they learn the play and serve themselves. Other genuine wealthy people should want you to grow and be successful.. It doesn't make them look good if those around aren't growing. For you attract that what you are. What You put out, You get back. You have to be highly intentional about what you are focused on, what you watch, and what you consume.

I've unfollowed those pages that aren't positive or motivating or no longer serve me or my purpose. I encourage you to do the same. Proverbs 13:20 says, "20 Walk with the wise and become wise, for a companion of fools suffers harm." Take a good, honest look in the mirror and ask yourself whether you know more about Beyonce and Jay Z or whatever celebrity that's out now than your own purpose.

Where is your mindset? Are you putting more energy into things and people that do not even know you exist, nor will they ever, if you do not live your life to its fullest potential? Find more ways to have real-life moments with real people in real life. Don't just watch others be successful. Get in on the action. Take an audit of your friends. What do they talk about? What are they into?

Decrease your time talking to and hanging out with people who aren't uplifting, encouraging, or motivating. Still love them. Never stop loving. But some things you have to do for yourself. Start getting in the right rooms showing up, and start listening more. You have to surround yourself with like-minded people, people who are living what they talk about. Find those who care about making a real impact. Get a mentor or a coach. I'm your coach in this book, but it's up to you to allow me to Coach you outside of this book. Find someone who motivates, encourages, inspires, and pulls greatness out of you.

After leaving Chicago, A friend of mine, a Mentor and big brother, a former youth pastor at our church growing up, asked me to lunch. We hadn't spoken in a while, and I used to be his co-host on his gospel radio show, 95.7 Gospel

Jamz with DJ Strick! Now Dr.Strick. I truly thank God for this man because he gave this young, hurt, broken, teenage girl something positive to do. He kept me off the streets. He taught me radio skills and hosting skills. He was the one who helped mold me into the persona ALowe. He believed in me and gave me a platform, which gave me a voice, which helped provide me with confidence in who I am.

I'm not sure if he is fully aware of all the pain I was holding on to back then, but he saw something in me that I didn't see in myself and allowed me to be on the radio – a privilege I took for granted. If I could go back, I would have done so much more with that opportunity. The show was highly successful. I believe Radio or another huge syndicated show will be in my future.

We went to lunch, and he reminded me of my passion and love for writing while talking. He reminded me that I had gotten in trouble once for writing up a school gossip paper and passing it around the school. I DID! It was called "The Scoop," and it was fire! It had all the news, like who was dating who and what teacher was trippin' with the homework that week. Honestly, I had forgotten how important writing was to me at that time. When I left lunch that day, I went home and started journaling again.

Through that process, this book came about. That's when I stopped writing affirmations. I started listening to God to hear what He wanted me to write. See all the pieces aligned. One thing I know this book is supposed to be.

I know I have shared so much and been around the world and sharing my story, but I pray you are encouraged along the journey. Sometimes it's not a simple point A to point B, but instead twists and turns and re-routing that actually get us where we were meant to be. Getting back or being around people who love and support you, genuinely want the best for you, inspire you, and people you can trust, getting back in church, and finding a team, are all pathways to purpose.

I started going live every day of the week at 6:15 am CST. I was going live on Instagram, Facebook, Youtube, and TikTok. My audience grew to thousands of people all over the world. I have family and friends I pray with, rejoice with, and cry with all over the world. I use my platform to connect with people. Find other believers. We are building a community of believers in every different field. I turned my Light on and found my Team.

When looking for your team, look for a place where You feel encouraged, motivated, and valued for Your gifts and abilities. 1 Corinthians 15:33 says, "Be not dismayed for bad company corrupts good character." If you're trying to be whole, You should not be hanging around people who no longer serve yo, who will not benefit you at all. You need to be around whole people. If you want to be successful, get around successful people. Do not seek to be the smartest in the room. Get around people who can teach you something, show you something, motivate you, and bring out the best in you. When they speak, listen, and pray if they are sent from God or sent to distract you from your assignment. Pray for discernment when seeking a team.

Lastly, trust the Coach and team that God has sent. Understand that they are the expert, they know more than you. Be willing to execute the plays and information that they provide. They are there to help you, so ask questions and do not be afraid to ask for help. Your coach or mentor has to be approachable. If you are afraid or feel like you can't to speak to them, you should find someone else.

Your best friend who is a coach may not be the best Coach or mentor for you, either. When looking for a coach, follow the person on social media. Pay attention to the content they post. What's their personality like? Does it vibe well with yours? Is this someone that you would like to have a conversation with? What is their business, and what do they do? How do they benefit your growth or empower your assignment? How can you serve? Can you serve under them? Choosing Real Talk Kim and Ash Cash as Mentors was a no-brainer for me at the time. And depending on what season of your life you are in, you will change teams. Need different coaches and mentors for the changing seasons in life.

Currently, I have a Marketing Coach and a Content Design Coach. I also partnered with my former Marketing Coach to create "Coach Launchers". To make sure You give your clients the best, make sure you are always learning and investing in yourself to give yourself, your family, and your clients the best version of you. Continue to seek God on who the right people should be to guide and partner with you. I have a community that you are invited to join. We are the **Trillionaire Mindset Family on Facebook.** If you go to www.TrillionairesOnly.com You will find us. At the time of this book, we are over 700 people deep. Just waiting on you.

What about your friends?

1.) Do You have a mentor or someone that you can seek for advice when it comes to life and business? Maybe it's a celebrity pastor or some famous motivational speaker. If yes, what qualities about them as a person made you want to learn from them? If no, what qualities would you like for your mentor to have?

_____

_____

_____

_____

_____

_____

_____

_____

_____

_____

_____

_____

_____

_____

_____

_____

2.) List Your friends. What qualities do you like about them? What qualities do You all have in common? I know you are a wonderful friend, but how could you better let your friends know that you appreciate them more?

_____

_____

_____

_____

_____

_____

_____

_____

_____

_____

_____

_____

_____

_____

_____

_____

_____

3.) What behaviors and traits are non-negotiable when having a friendship with you?

_____
_____
_____
_____
_____
_____
_____
_____
_____
_____
_____
_____
_____
_____
_____
_____
_____
_____
_____
_____
_____

Let's Pray:

Dear Lord,

Thank You, Great King, for loving us so much that You sent people here to do life alongside us. Thank You for our family, our spouses, and the people You have given us to be our teammates through life's many ups and downs. Thank You, Father, for our friendships. Please allow the right friendships to continue to bloom and grow. Protect us, Father, from the wolves in sheep's clothing who do not mean us any good. Send us the right mentors and coaches You ordained to speak into our lives to guide us down the path You have for us. Remind us when life hits that it's not good to be alone. Remind us daily that we are here for each other. Heal our brokenness or whatever we need to find a team where we fit in, serve, and thrive.

In Jesus' Name,

Amen

Affirm These:

1.) I can accomplish anything.
2.) I am full of energy and great ideas.
3.) I am open to God-aligned friendships and business partnerships.
4.) I am friendly, so I attract other friendly people.
5.) I am a significant contributor to my family, tribe, and community.
6.) I am love. I attract more of what I am.
7.) I release those things and people who no longer serve me.

(Write these out in the space below)

Strategy #6

Give Your Testimony

It's on you to share the story after all, has been said and done. After you have entirely given that care, worry, trial, situation, heartbreak, disappointment, whatever, over to God, you have a responsibility. Speak of the Goodness of God and share with as many as you can. Remember, we are to help others. It isn't about us. We were allowed to go down that path to be entrusted with the assignment to bring others to deliverance. It is a serious task, but God would not have sent us here if He didn't think that we were more than capable of being a being light bearers, of being different, of being honest and willing to share with those who God will send to you to ask what's so different about your life. Why do you have so much joy? What medicine healed you?

Jesus just wants You to tell the truth. It was Him that saved you. He just wants the credit. Here is the thing, when you put it on God, now it's on Him. Now its on His name, and His name is the healer. He will not let you have anything wrong to say about His name. For His Namesake He will show up and out as the ultimate healer He is

Sharing your testimony is the thing that will lead others to Christ.Whenever we are looking to purchase anything, it could be a new shirt, shoes, a new course, investing in some stock, whatever, if we make an investment, we will ensure we research it. We go straight to the reviews to see how the product worked for others. Same thing with our faith. Others want to see how God works in Your life.

Others want to know what you have personally experienced regarding God. When You share your Triumph story, you encourage them and encourage you because you get reminded of how God stepped in for you. The Bible says that He is the same God that He changes not. So if He has delivered before, He will again, and He is no respecter of persons, so He will work for You and whoever calls upon His name, just like that Leaper.

In Revelations 12:11 (KJV), the Bible says, "they are overcome by the blood of the Lamb. And by the word of their testimony." I didn't realize it but by opening up and speaking out about me being molested, raped, having miscarriages, being rejected, hated on, lied on, broken. It freed me. It released me. It was so freeing to just get it out. And it not only helped me, but I had no idea how many women were encouraged by my openness and willingness to share. The enemy has a way of making us feel isolated. It was never God's design for us to be alone, so that's why the enemy encourages it so much.

When things happen, you first think you are alone and no one understands your pain. 1 Corinthians 10:13 says, "No temptation has overtaken you except what is common to mankind. And God is faithful; he will not let you be tempted beyond what you can bear. But when you are tempted, he will also provide a way out so that you can endure it." That verse is so rich. What you are going through, someone else has gone through, and there will be others to go through it too.

We all face the same trials in life; we all have choices. If you could have had someone tell you don't go down that way because there is a big hole in the sidewalk, wouldn't you consider that valuable information? God put us on assignment to help others along our path. We aren't supposed to set up a tent, however. You keep going and sharing what you learn as you go. I believe that is the whole point of life. We are supposed to go live our life boldly for God, being the light that He has created us to be. We are supposed to use our gifts to make a difference in our homes and communities. When we display greatness, and others ask what gave us hope, strength, and endurance to achieve our goals, God just wants the truth. It was because God made a way. It was because God came through. It was because God opened a door. It was because He healed. That's it. He wants you to give Him the glory. He wants the testimonial. He wants the review. He is definitely well deserving.

The latter part of that last scripture says, but when you are tempted, He will also provide a way out so you can endure it. He loves us so much that He is always giving us opportunities to make the best decisions for our lives. Others need to know that God will help them out of their temptations. Others need to know that they are not alone, that others have gone through that same pain too but survived. They need to see not just what surviving looks like but what it looks like to thrive. We are all surviving. But they will never know what thriving looks like if you never open your mouth and share about the peace and joy that God can bring.

Philippians 1:12, " *Now I want you to know, brothers and sisters, that what has happened to me has actually served to advance the gospel.*" Everything that happens to you serves a purpose. **Romans 8:28** says, *"And we know that in all things God works for the good of those who love him, who have been called according to his purpose."* It was all for the glory of God. Your story is yours, no one can take it from you, and God has completely written it. So it's perfect!

You don't have to speak about anything that you do not know. You are the expert on your story. You do not have to overthink your witness. You just need to be honest. Speak on your life before Christ. Your introduction to Christ and how your life has been now. As you share with others, You will be reminded and encouraged. 2 Corinthians 1:4 says, "who comforts us in all our troubles, so that we can comfort those in any trouble with the comfort we receive from God." We receive comfort from God so that we can comfort others.

This life will hit all of us. We were promised that we would have trials. Your story can give hope and encouragement to others and yourself. Take your time. Find someone that you feel comfortable sharing with. A trustworthy praying friend, a minister, try therapy, journal.

Find some way to get out how you are feeling. Releasing it physically is freeing. I have written letters to people that they will never read because they are burned, ripped up, or deleted. I never wrote them with the intent of anyone reading them. I wrote them to free my thoughts and emotions. Writing became and is my therapy. My release. My catharsis.

My love for writing started after that thing had happened. If it had not been for those awful experiences, you would not be reading this book right now. I have grown to see that God had a plan, even in that situation too. He knew you would be holding this book and needed this story to be encouraged and inspired. He knew that you needed to know (through my story) that even though things are considered bad sometimes, things beyond your control happen, and they suck, and it's hard, but you will still overcome and be okay. You can and will smile again. As joint heirs with Christ, Triumph is ours. The choice to walk and share boldly in that truth is yours.

Let's dig deeper...

1.) What was Your life like before Christ? What was it that brought you to the faith? What Changes have you noticed since having Christ in Your life?

_____

_____

_____

_____

_____

_____

_____

_____

_____

_____

_____

_____

_____

_____

_____

_____

_____

_____

2.) If You were asked to share your testimony in the next few moments, would you be able to? Yes or No? What part of Your story would you tell? If the person does not believe in God, will that upset you? Be honest.

_____

_____

_____

_____

_____

_____

_____

_____

_____

_____

_____

_____

_____

_____

_____

_____

_____

_____

_____

3.) What is one of your favorite attributes about God? (Waymaker, Healer, Deliverer, Secret Keeper) Why? Would you Share this with a friend?

_____

_____

_____

_____

_____

_____

_____

_____

_____

_____

_____

_____

_____

_____

_____

_____

Let's Pray:

Dear Lord,

Thank You for our stories. Thank You for the life that You have granted us to live. We trust You in every area of our life, including what we are uneasy about and the things that hurt us. We will trust that You have a plan for those things too. Help us to see the lessons. Thank You for giving us wisdom, insight, and most importantly, victory. We know we can do all things through You. Send us those who align with our stories. Thank You for every life connected to us. Remind us that we were assigned to prove that you exist by doing what You do. Be God in our lives. We trust You. Forgive us for not speaking up more when we had the opportunity. Moving forward, we will commit to being the light that You have created us to be.

In Jesus' Name,

Amen

Affirm These:

1.) I have a powerful story.
2.) I am a beacon of hope for those who can relate to my story.
3.) I am open to sharing the beautiful things God has done in my life.
4.) I am sure that God didn't bring me this far to leave me.
5.) I am confident God has a plan for my life and my story.
6.) I am in abundance because He has blessed me abundantly.
7.) My voice matters.

(Write this out in the space below)

Strategy #7

Get to Work

Finally, the last play in the Triumph Playbook. The shortest chapter because the message is simple: Now it's time to get to work. the Bible says that Faith without works is dead. You have work to do! It's time to set a real plan of action. First things first, you now have to decide. How will you go about shining your light? Think of the most impactful thing that you can do for the Kingdom. Is it writing that book? Starting that business? Going into the ministry? What can you do for Christ? Hak 2:2 says, "Write the vision down and make it plain that those who read it may run with it." Listen, success is never an accident. It's more likely to come to those who have a plan for it. So write down your plan.

One of the benefits of working on your God-given purpose and assignment is that it gives you a sense of direction and meaning in life. When you know what you were created to do, you can focus your energy and resources on the things that matter most to you. You can avoid distractions and make better decisions about how to spend your time and energy. This sense of direction and purpose can be a guiding light in times of uncertainty and challenges.

Another benefit of working on your God-given purpose and assignment is that it can bring you fulfillment and satisfaction. When doing work that aligns with your values and strengths, you are likelier to feel a sense of purpose and accomplishment. This can lead to greater happiness and well-being in your life. Pursuing your God-given purpose and assignment can help you live a more fulfilling life.

In addition to personal fulfillment, pursuing your God-given purpose and assignment can positively impact others. When you use your gifts and talents to serve others, you can make a meaningful difference in their lives. This can bring you a sense of satisfaction and joy, knowing that you are positively impacting the world. Pursuing your God-given purpose and assignment can help you contribute to a better world.

Ultimately, working on your God-given purpose and assignment is vital because it allows you to live authentically to who you are and what you believe in. It can help you find meaning, fulfillment, and purpose and positively impact your world. When you live a life of authenticity, you are happier and more fulfilled and inspire others to do the same.

Getting to work on your God-given purpose and assignment is not just a religious concept but a practical one. It can help you find direction, fulfillment, and meaning while positively impacting others. It is always possible to discover your purpose and start pursuing it. Take the first step today and see how it transforms your life.

1.)What are your gifts and talents? What comes easy to you and harder to others? What do people usually seek your advice on?

_____

_____

_____

_____

_____

_____

_____

_____

_____

2.)List 3 ways for each gift and talent listed above how they can all be used for the betterment of the Kingdom?

_____

_____

_____

_____

_____

_____

_____

_____

_____

Let's Pray

I lift up the reader of this prayer to You now. Thank You for equipping us with all the tools we need to succeed. Thank You for your guidance and clear instructions on how we are to execute your plans. Be with them and their plans. You said you would bless the work of our hands, so bless their plans and minds with ideas and creativity that will advance the Kingdom and their mindset, and help them excel in life. Thank You for Your plan to give us Victory. Remind us always that we win in the end. Thank You for Your faithfulness. To You be all the glory and honor. In Your name we pray, Amen.

Affirm These:

1.) My plans are blessed.
2.) My plans will prospers.
3.) God wants me to prosper.
4.) I am victorious.
5.) Any plans against the plan God has for me will not prosper.
6.) I am chosen to be Great.
7.) I am anointed for victory.

(Write this out in the space below)

Final Run Through

Isaiah 41:10 says, "*Fear not, for I am with you. Be not dismayed, for I am your God; I will strengthen you, help you; I will uphold you with my righteous right hand.*" Not only is this one of my favorite scriptures, but it's also the truth. I feel these words because I have felt His presence. Nobody's life is perfect, even though things may look perfect on the outside. Perfect life or not, no one is exempt from hardships. **Matthew 5:45** says, "*... He causes his sun to rise on the evil and the good, and sends rain on the righteous and the unrighteous.*"

Trials happen, but they are all allowed by God. They may not make sense, but You have to trust in His plan. **Jeremiah 29:11** says, " *'For I know the plans I have for you,'*" declares the Lord, "'* plans to prosper you and not to harm you, plans to give you hope and a future.'*" God didn't just create you just to torture you. He made You so He could use your life as an example to lead the lost to Him. You were chosen.

I'm going to remind you as I did in the beginning. Especially if you made it to this point, it is no coincidence that you found this book that you read this book. God has a great purpose and design for Your life. **Proverbs 18:16** says, *"A man's gift makes room for him, And brings him before great men."* God has blessed you with something so uniquely special.

You are different for a reason. You don't fit in because you were born to stand out. To be You confidently, whoever God created, boldly and unashamed for Him. It starts with understanding that life will challenge you. Remember **John 16:33**, *"I have told you these things, so that in me you may have peace. In this world, you will have trouble. But take heart! I have overcome the world."* You could focus on the first part of the scripture or stand firm on the latter part.... "But Take Heart! I have overcome the world." No matter what happens or how it looks, God and His people will win. Trust God. Trust God. Trust God. & and you will Triumph.

Let's recap the strategies, Number 1 Get Over Being Hurt. You cannot heal what you do not reveal. Embrace the hurts and the traumas, and most importantly, embrace your healing! Secondly, give it to God. The loads that are heavy to us are light to Him. Embrace your load bearer. Third, Get up. Just because you went through a rough patch, you don't have to stay there – embrace the purpose waiting on the other side of this for you. You didn't go through all of that for nothing. Fourth, Give God praise. Remembering who you are is paramount. Embrace God, knowing that He has never left you, nor will he forsake you. EVER! Fifth, Get a Team. Embrace the power of togetherness. Also, **Hebrews 10:25** says, " *And let us not neglect our meeting together, as some people do, but encourage one another, especially now that the day of his return is drawing near.* " We need each other. Sixth and last key, Give your testimony. Embrace and share your story so that God can get the glory.

Finally, I want to leave you with the Message version of **2 Corinthians 4:8-18**, *"If you only look at us, you might well miss the brightness. We carry this precious Message around in the unadorned clay pots of our ordinary lives. That's to prevent anyone from confusing God's incomparable power with us. As it is, there's not much chance of that. You know for yourselves that we're not much to look at. We've been surrounded and battered by troubles, but we're not demoralized; we're not sure what to do, but we know that God knows what to do; we've been spiritually terrorized, but God hasn't left our side; we've been thrown down, but we haven't broken. What they did to Jesus, they do to us—trial and torture, mockery and murder; what Jesus did among them, he does in us—he lives! Our* *lives are at constant risk for Jesus' sake, which makes Jesus' life all the more evident in us. While we're going through the worst, you're getting in on the best!*

13–15 We're not keeping this quiet, not on your life. Just like the psalmist who wrote, "I believed it, so I said it," we say what we believe. And what we believe is that the One who raised up the Master Jesus will just as certainly raise us up with you, alive. Every detail works to your advantage and to God's glory: more and more grace, more and more people, more and more praise!

16–18 So we're not giving up. How could we! Even though on the outside it often looks like things are falling apart on us, on the inside, where God is making new life, not a day goes by without his unfolding grace. These hard times are small potatoes compared to the coming good times, the lavish celebration prepared for us. There's far more here than meets the eye. The things we see now are here today, gone tomorrow. But the things we can't see now will last forever."

If this book has been a blessing to you, please share these words so that they may be an encouragement to someone else. Maybe you aren't ready to share your story. You have my permission to share mine. I am the Trillion

Dollar Lady, but it's because I am trying to fill my heavenly account up with as many souls as possible before He calls me home. I want to encourage as many of you as possible. I want you to know. You can be free. Not to give up but to GET UP. Let's help as many moves towards wholeness and trust God with confidence.

This is the last write-in section of the book. I asked a bit more and gave a bit more. Continue to answer honestly. Also, please let's keep in touch.

Text "Trillions" to (205) 858-4099 to keep in touch. I will never spam you, but if you have prayer requests, you can text, and I will send out motivational words, affirmations, and scriptures. It's free. I look forward to encouraging you further. If you would be interested in taking the coaching beyond these pages. Go to www.Coachlaunchers.com and book a free call to speak with me. I want you great! Now the real work begins.

1.) What Great Thing has God done in Your life in the last 3 months? Last week? Do you believe that there is a testimony in each day? Why or why not?

_____

_____

_____

_____

_____

_____

_____

_____

_____

_____

_____

_____

_____

_____

_____

2.) If this were the last day on earth would you be pleased with how you spent it? Would You be confident that You would be in line waiting to hear, "Well Done!"

_____

_____

_____

_____

_____

_____

_____

_____

_____

3.) Matthew 6:19-21 talks about storing up for Yourself treasures in heaven. How do you think You can do that? What do you believe is your current heavenly balance?

_____

_____

_____

_____

_____

_____

_____

_____

_____

4.) Write a letter to your future self Congratulating Yourself on whatever you want to achieve by whatever time You want to achieve it by. For example, "Hey ALowe, Boo Congratulations on speaking at that 100,000 seat arena, Congrats on that new house. Congrats on 20 years of marriage, to Your College Sweetheart Matt McCants.... etc etc Now Your turn. Remember this is Your book Dream as little or as big as you like. Habakkuk 2:2 says, "...Write down the revelation and make it plain..."

_____

_____

_____

_____

_____

_____

_____

_____

_____

_____

_____

_____

_____

5.) Proverbs 29:18 says, "Where there is no vision, the people perish: but he that keepeth the law, happy is he." You have your vision but how are You going to make those things happen that You see for yourself? What work will you do? How will you do it? Who will help you do it. Map it out. You have to know where you are going and how you will get there.

I will write a book and sale a million copies. I will hire a marketing team to help me get my book out,I will raise the funds by.._____

_____

_____

_____

_____

_____

_____

_____

_____

_____

_____

_____

6.)Do you feel ready to step out of the shadows to live your life boldly and confidently for the King of Kings? What is Your biggest take away from this book? How has this book helped you?

_____

_____

_____

_____

_____

_____

_____

_____

_____

_____

_____

_____

_____

_____

Will you share your takeaway with me? I would love to hear your thoughts and celebrate your wins. Reach out to me on all platforms as @its.alowe Dm me.

Lets Pray:

Dear Heavenly Father. Thank You to the person holding this book, the person reading these pages right now. I pray they have been blessed by the words You have given me on these pages. If they're still having a hard time dealing with any brokenness or hardships, help them to be able to use and apply the 7 steps that You have given me to heal and triumph. Watch over them and keep them. Uplift them with Your mighty right hand. Cover them with Your love. As they read this, begin to fill them with peace and reassurance. Give them hope that if You allow something, it must be working for their good. Thank You that hardships do not last forever and that You promised to be our friend when difficulties come. I thank You for our stories and lift up those who have hurt us. I lift them up to You. I pray for their lives, that they come to know you like never before. I thank you for choosing us for Your glory. We trust you with it all. We will continue the race strong towards Triumph knowing that You are for us. Thank You Father, In Jesus' name, Amen.

Affirm These:
Look up the Missing Scriptures. Write them in the blanks.

All things are working together for my good

"And we know that in all things God works for the good of those who love him, who have been called according to his purpose."

– Romans 8:28

I am Healed

"But He was wounded for our transgressions, He was bruised for our iniquities; The chastisement for our peace was upon Him, And by His stripes, we are healed." Isaiah 53:5

God is a healer and He desires for me to be healed.

" He said, "If you listen carefully to the Lord your God and do what is right in his eyes, if you pay attention to his commands and keep all his decrees, I will not bring on you any of the diseases I brought on the Egyptians, for I am the Lord, who heals you." – Exodus 15:26

The Lord restores and heals me back to full health

"But I will restore you to health and heal your
wounds,'

declares the Lord...." - Jeremiah 30:17

I am protected.

_____

_____

_____

_____

_____

_____

_____

_____

_____ - Psalms 91:7

I serve an awesome God who promises to never leave or forsake me.

_____
_____
_____
_____
_____
_____
_____
_____
_____
_____ –

Deuteronomy 31:6

I am a New Creation in Christ Jesus.

_____
_____
_____
_____
_____
_____ – 2

Corinthians 5:17

Happy Winning! I am so proud of You! You are going to do great things I know it! It's giving Triumph!!

It's a Great Day to Have a Great Day!! Choose it! NOW RUN THE PLAY!

For more information

@its.alowe

For those that are seeking Salvation

If you do not know Jesus Christ as your Personal Lord and Savior or would like to rededicate your life to Him. Romans 10:9 says, "If you declare with your mouth, "Jesus is Lord," and believe in your heart that God raised him from the dead, you will be saved." It truly is simple. Read this prayer below and if you agree, pray it out loud to receive Our Savior into your life.

Prayer for Salvation

"Lord Jesus, I confess my sins and ask for your forgiveness. Please come into my heart as my Lord and Savior. Take complete control of my life and help me to walk in Your footsteps daily by the power of the Holy Spirit. Thank you Lord for saving me and for answering my prayer. In Jesus' name. Amen."

Welcome to the Kingdom of God!!

If that was Your first time praying that prayer or if you would like more information on the faith please reach out to a local church. Don't have one? Reach out to us.

https://www.guidinglight.org/salvation/

www.ingramcontent.com/pod-product-compliance
Lightning Source LLC
La Vergne TN
LVHW051243080426
835513LV00016B/1720